pass the
peanut butter
and *jelly*

pass the
peanut butter
and *jelly*
inspirational stories
for sandwiched families

Dr. Beth Robinson

COVENANT
PUBLISHING

www.covenantpublishing.com

P.O. Box 390 Webb City, Missouri 64870
Call toll free at 877.673.1015

Library of Congress Cataloging-in-Publication Data
Robinson, Beth, 1964-
 Pass the peanut butter and jelly : inspirational stories for sandwiched families /
Beth Robinson.
     p. cm.
 ISBN 1-892435-48-9 (pbk.)
 1. Sandwich generation—Religious life. 2. Robinson, Beth, 1964- I. Title.
 BV4579.5.R64 2005
 248.4--dc22
                                   2005007528

This book is dedicated to my mom and dad

who instilled in me a faith in God

that continues to guide me and inspire me daily.

The words "Be happy, well, and faithful to God"

challenge me every day.

Jean –
i appreciate your
passion for CCU. It
excites me to work
with you! Take care
of yourself!
Beth

acknowledgments

I am deeply grateful that I have the privilege of sharing my daily life with Christi, Treca, Sarah, and Gerrit. They continually encourage me to write and to find ways to use my talents to serve God. My life is enriched by knowing them and by sharing our daily struggles together.

As you read this book, you will come to recognize what a tremendous influence and inspiration both my parents and grandparents have been in my life. The stories I share in this book are told from the perspective of a child and a grandchild. To the best of my ability I have tried to be accurate in my recollection of situations, but truthfully my perspective as the child and grandchild influence how I see all the events described in this book. For those of you who know or knew my parents or grandparents, please accept my apologies for any inaccuracies that may exist. I am telling these stories from my limited perspective. These stories have continued to shape my actions and my identity throughout my lifetime, and they are told with humility and gratitude for how the experiences shaped who I am and will be.

God is remarkable. He has brought just the right people into my life to encourage me to pursue my writing. Susan Blassingame has harassed me unmercifully for nearly twelve years to write this book. In hindsight, I don't think I would ever have written this without her nudging and prodding. She graciously helped edit the rough drafts of these stories and made insightful comments to help improve them immensely. I owe you one, Susan. Thanks for your help.

I continually thank God for bringing Steve Cable, John Hunter, and Covenant Publishing into my life. I am humbled by working with two Godly men who are seeking God's will in their lives and business. Thanks for your continued support.

It doesn't matter
who my father was;
it matters who
I remember he was.

–Anne Sexton

table of contents

1 *pass the peanut butter and jelly* Page 11

2 *blue skies and dirty dishes* Page 25

3 *the reading room* Page 37

4 *trashed treasures* Page 49

5 *snow's a comin'* Page 61

6 *taking turns* Page 73

7 *rub-a-dub-dub* Page 85

8 *pieces of memories* Page 97

9 *now i lay me down to sleep* Page 109

10 *recipe for respect* Page 121

11 *grandma's blessing* Page 133

12 *taking my turn* Page 145

about the author Page 157

How far you go in life

depends on your being tender with the young,

compassionate with the aged,

sympathetic with the striving,

and tolerant of the weak and strong.

Because some day in your life

you will have been all of these.

–George Washington Carver

1
pass the
peanut butter
and *jelly*

*Our main business is
not to see what lies
dimly in the distance
but to do what lies
clearly at hand.*

–Thomas Carlyle

Sandwich generation? What an interesting term for people who are caring for their children and their parents at the same time. In fact, people who care for their children, their aging parents, and their aging grandparents are club sandwiches! Sandwich generation refers to the dilemma of meeting the needs and desires of two generations. Sandwiched . . . one generation on one side of you and another generation on the other side of you. Sandwiched . . . pulled in two different directions.

Divided loyalties.
Divided time.
Divided energy.

You are split between the roles of being a child and being a parent. You feel double guilt because you aren't devoting enough attention to being a parent or to being a child. You are utterly confused.

Divided loyalties.
Divided time.
Divided energy.

Are you wondering who has to pay the price—your kids or your parents? Slow down a minute. Take a deep breath. Relax.

Maybe no one has to "pay a price." Being sandwiched isn't easy, but it doesn't mean you have to say no to either your parents or your children. Even though you are sandwiched, you can say yes to both your parents and your children. Although I am not sandwiched yet, I'm standing on the edge of the sandwich journey with kids in my home and parents who are aging. I know you can say yes to both your parents and your children, because I had parents who said yes to me and to my grandparents. Being sandwiched was challenging for my parents. They dealt with confusion and frustration.

Divided loyalties.
Divided time.
Divided energy.

Despite the confusion and frustration, my parents navigated raising four children while being the primary caregivers for my mother's parents. My parents were ordinary people who rose to extraordinary heights to care for my grandparents. Maybe one of the reasons my parents were so effective in dealing with being sandwiched is because they came from such different backgrounds and had such different perspectives on the world.

Years after leaving the family farm where he was raised, dad continued to cling to the farm values and culture. Dad was always more comfortable in work clothes than in dress clothes. Every chance he got, he pulled on lace up work boots and went to check cattle, build fence, or pick up a hammer. He was employed as a school administrator who did way too much of everything and was good at it all. He was the business manager, the tax collector, the director of transportation, the director of maintenance, purchasing agent, and the construction supervisor (and probably several other things as well). Dad was extraordinary because he was a blue-collar man who found success and fulfillment in a white-collar work world.

My dad stood 6'2" tall and was bigger than life. He had big hands, a big stride, and a big heart. When he graduated from high school he had thick wavy dark hair, but most of his hair fell out while he was being shipped to Korea during the Korean War. My memories of my dad are of a tall, broad shoulder man who had callused hands and skin tattooed by wind and sun. Dad had a wicked sense of humor and loved practical jokes, yet we rarely saw him smile. When dad was five, he was pulling on the tail of horse named Susie and the horse got more than a little irritated and let a hoof fly that caught dad in the mouth. That hoof knocked out dad's two front teeth. Dad was never able to have those teeth replaced.

While dad was terrorizing animals on the farm as a kid, mom was struggling to develop a sense of identity in a family where she perceived that she embarrassed my grandma. During the birth process, mom's arm was twisted and a well-meaning doctor put a splint on her arm to help it heal. However, as a result of that splint, my mom's range of motion in her right arm never developed correctly. My mom has no motion in her right elbow and using her right arm draws attention to her disability. Grandma didn't like for my mother to sweep or take care of other household chores because mom's arm looked awkward when she tried to complete chores. My mom believed that my grandma was ashamed of her. Ironically, none of us kids even realized my mom's arm was injured until we were nearly adults.

Mom grew up exceeding expectations in every way possible. She started school a year early, skipped a grade in elementary school, finished high school in three years, and then finished college in three years. By the time my mom was 19 years old she had a college diploma and a teaching certificate. My granddad drove my mom to Stinnett and left her there to start her first teaching job while she was still a teenager herself. My mom was still teaching in that same school district when my dad moved there six years later. My dad convinced my mom to skip a parent teacher association meeting and go on a date with him. Although mom took off a few years to have kids, she only taught in one school system during her career.

Even after my parents married, my mom remained remarkably independent. Mom had her checking account and dad had his checking account. In fact, mom generally managed the money and most of the people in the household. Mom managed to provide Band-Aids, baths, and bedtime stories to all four of us kids. A remarkable feat when you realize there are only five and a half years between the birth of the oldest child and youngest child. Despite surgeries, inner ear difficulties, migraines, and a heart murmur, mom always had a listening ear and time for a hug.

As parents, while dad emphasized work boots and work ethic, mom emphasized etiquette, appropriate clothing, and diverse educational experiences. Dad made sure we knew how to herd cattle and drive a nail, while mom made sure that we heard classical music and learned how to set the table for a formal meal. When we needed help with homework, dad helped with math and science, while mom helped with English and reading.

When my granddad had a stroke, all of us kids were involved in sports and still demanding a lot of mom's time and energy. Mom was our chauffeur, our counselor, our tutor, our cook, and our stability. We had just returned from a baseball game on a summer's evening when my grandma called about my granddad having a stroke. That phone call changed our family life drastically, and it never resumed in quite the same way again.

The summer of the stroke was spent dealing with the crisis aspects of the situation. While my mom was out of school for the summer, my dad was snowed under with reconciling the end of the year budget and with overseeing the summer maintenance program at the school. Dad stayed for the first week after the stroke, but his job demanded that he return to work. For the rest of that summer, my family was split into two family units. Two kids stayed with my mom as she helped care for her parents, and two kids stayed at home with my dad while he worked. My dad would commute on the weekends to my grandparents' house to help. Mom's brothers and sisters came in and out during the summer to help. For several weeks, someone had to sit with my granddad around the clock at the hospital, so it took a lot of manpower to take care of him. The adults all took night shifts, but we kids would fill in for a few hours during the day so the adults could rest. Now as an adult, I don't know how my parents handled all the stressors of that summer.

By the end of the summer, my aunts and uncles had to return to their homes and lives, while someone had to help my grandparents. By the time school started in the fall, they moved my granddad from the hospital to a nursing home for rehabilitation. My mom went back to her job as a teacher, and continued to commute to my grandparents' house every weekend. Although my granddad was still bedridden, my grandma insisted that she could take care of my granddad at home when he was released from rehab. Although my parents had concerns about my grandma's ability to take care of my granddad, they worked diligently to help get my grandparent's house set up for my granddad to return home.

Once grandma brought granddad home, it was immediately evident that she could not care for him by herself. My granddad had to be lifted in and out of the bed, and he had to be strapped into a wheelchair to move him from room to room. My grandma had to feed him, bathe him, and get him a bedpan. Grandma was forced to admit that she could not cope with the situation by herself. The decision was made that grandma and granddad would move to Stinnett, so my parents could help take care of them. In addition to caring for my grandparents, my parents now had to oversee cleaning out grandma's house and selling the house and some rental properties as well. Mom and dad continued to commute to my grandparents' house on the weekends. Dad began to build a house across the street from our house for my grandparents to live in. While dad built the house, grandma and granddad moved into a rent house that we owned on the other side of town. Thus began our first taste of peanut butter and jelly.

For several years I had a front row seat watching how my parents coped with being sandwiched. My granddad lived for three years after the initial stroke. He was paralyzed on one side of his body and required a great deal of physical care. My grandma was diabetic, and she lived for thirteen years after my granddad's first stroke.

From my front row seat I learned . . .

* Faith is more important than finances.

* Peanut butter, mustard, and pickle sandwiches are a complete meal.

* Loving someone can be exhausting and frustrating.

* Reds and whites aren't a good combination for laundry.

* Tears aren't always bad.

* Wearing a wig backwards makes a definite fashion statement.

* Nobody wants to clean the toilets.

* Chaos is a form of landscaping.

* Being a servant is what you do when no one outside your family acknowledges it.

* Bodies decay, but souls are eternal.

At a family reunion a few years ago, I was talking with my cousins and realized many of them didn't have a close relationship with my grandparents. In fact, they really didn't even know my grand-parents. They never had the opportunity to know their own family history and the legacy of my grandparents. As a result, my cousins missed out on . . .

* The warm, funny, totally zany moments of living in the altered reality of a grandparent who has had a stroke

* The frustrations of trying to negotiate life with grandma and her sense of thriftiness

* The rare moments of hearing poems recited from memory

* The quiet moments of shared solitude sitting by a hospital bed

* The triumph of completing a quilt with grandma

* The grasp of a grandparent's hand seeking comfort from some-one familiar

My parents gave me the irreplaceable gift of having a close, per-sonal relationship with my grandparents. Admittedly, my parents paid a high cost to provide that opportunity for me. The good moments were accompanied by lots of struggles and frustrations. Physical and emotional exhaustion joined family gatherings. I knew at a young age what it was for another human soul to totally depend on you for care. My parents missed moments of relaxation and even moments of our lives at times. Yet, observing my parents care for my grandparents was a blessing and a memorable legacy.

Unknowingly, my parents taught us some of the greatest lessons of spiritual devotion and service when they were washing out bed-pans and changing soiled linens. My parents still don't recognize what a positive impact their devotion to my grandparents has made on the lives of the kids on the other side of the sandwich. My mom still occasionally apologizes to us for "neglecting" us when we were kids because she was caring for her parents. No matter what I say to my mom, she doesn't seem to understand the positive impact her devotion to her parents had on me.

One of the greatest legacies of caring for my grandparents was the deepening of spiritual faith. As a young child, I snuggled up against my granddad while he read his Bible and held my grandma's hand on the way to Bible class. I sang church songs with them and climbed over both of them during worship services. As I got older, I observed the hospitality of my grandparents and their commitment to caring for other people, but nothing impacted me like helping care for my grandparents in their last years.

Witnessing the physical decline of my grandparents provided a rare window into how faith impacts and influences the final years and days of life. I heard my granddad beg God to let him die so he could go home. Years later, my granddad's pleadings echo in my mind . . . what a powerful understanding of the yearning to go home. As I get older, I appreciate more and more that longing to go home myself. I understand the common faith I share with my granddad. My spiritual faith grew in the environment of a sandwiched family.

Sandwiched? My parents were sandwiched. Like other sandwiched parents, they had a choice to make about what kind of sandwich they would create. They could have created a cold liver sandwich that would have left a bad taste in our mouths for years. But they didn't. They recognized that even when sandwiched, they could create something special for their children. Even as a kid, I recognized that mom and dad were the peanut butter and jelly in the middle of the sandwich. They took the middle position, caught between parents and children, and turned it into a positive experience. They took a challenging situation and forged a family legacy of concern and compassion. The stories in this book are snippets of life in a sandwiched family. They are the moments that built the family legacy.

As a child standing on the brink of being a member of the sandwiched generation, I recognize that my parents have equipped me well for the next stage of life. When I am sandwiched, I'll reach for the peanut butter and jelly.

the peanut butter

None of us wish for our parents to reach the point where they need our daily assistance to survive. Yet through the experiences of caring for both children and parents, God can refine us. Our faith is developed through trials.

When the church was located in Jerusalem, and before the persecutions arose, there began to be discontent, unrest, and allegations of neglect (Acts 6:1-4). When the persecutions, threats, and ravaging of the church began after the death of Stephen (Acts 8:1; 9:1) the church changed.

During these challenges and turmoil, we read in Acts 9:31, "Then the church throughout Judea, Galilee and Samaria enjoyed a time of peace. It was strengthened; and encouraged by the Holy Spirit, it grew in numbers, living in the fear of the Lord." Amazing peace, comfort, edification, and numerical growth—all during a time of persecution and suffering!

Faith under fire is refined and purified just like gold and other precious metals (1 Pet. 1:6-7). During this time I observed the faith of my parents and grandparents put to the test, "fired up" by adversity, illness, and physical limitation, but their refined and purified faith still shines for me today as a beacon showing the way through trials.

–ADAPTED FROM RANDALL MORRIS

the jelly

1. Our faith is refined by trials (1 Pet. 1:6-7). Describe times when you know that your faith has been refined by trials.

2. Describe how you think being "sandwiched" can strengthen your faith.

3. As Timothy learned his faith from his mother and grand-mother (2 Tim. 1:5), our children can learn about God through the way we deal with daily stressors. What do you want your children to learn from seeing you take care of your parents?

4. Frequently, we focus our eyes on the temporary rather than the eternal. We see dirty dishes, soiled sheets, and fragile bodies, while God wants us to see the souls of others. What can you do to keep your focus on God and his desire for your life?

the bread

In this you greatly rejoice,

though now for a little while

you may have had to suffer grief

in all kinds of trials.

These have come so that your faith

—of greater worth than gold,

which perishes even though refined by fire

—may be proved genuine and

may result in praise, glory and honor

when Jesus Christ is revealed

—1 PETER 1:6-7

Let the refining and improving
of your own life keep you so busy
that you have little time
to criticize others.

–H. Jackson Brown Jr.

2

blue skies and *dirty dishes*

Some days there won't be

a song in your heart.

Sing anyway.

–Emory Austin

Blue skies and rainbows and sunbeams from heaven . . .
Plates clang together before slipping under the water.

Are what I can see when my Lord is living in me . . .
Water gushes out of the spigot to rinse dishes.

I know that Jesus is well and alive today . . .
Two kids jostle together, reaching for dishes to dry.

He makes his home in my heart . . .
Knives, forks, and spoons clatter.

Never more will I be all alone . . .
Pots and pans compete for attention.

Since he promised me that we never would part.

Singing and doing dishes is a well-practiced ritual at my grandma's house.

Today there is a little bit more of a sense of urgency. Earlier in the day, grandma called to tell us that my granddad had had a stroke. We immediately loaded the car and drove the 75 miles to grandma's house. Now we are cleaning grandma's house before my uncles, aunts, and cousins arrive. While visiting grandma's house is always a great adventure for a kid, it comes at a cost. The cost for entry into the adventure is sweat equity.

Grandma's house swims with wonderful, musty rooms filled with all kinds of wonders and treasures. Her closets tuck boxes into angles and arches. Dust disguises shelves filled with intriguing books. General disorder dominates every room, but nothing competes with the confusion of the kitchen. The overwhelming chaos shouts that it is my grandma's kitchen.

Grandma loves to cook. She spends hours a day in the kitchen. She takes ownership of the kitchen like a general commandeering his troops. Without a glance at a recipe, her hands fly through kitchen cabinets retrieving ingredients, bowls, spoons, and pans. Without effort, her fingers open canisters, bottles, and jars. She deftly arranges ingredients in layers and bowls. A handful of this, a pinch of that, and a dab of fat synchronize in their own unique dance.

Grandma's ad-lib style of cooking distinguishes her at church. Men line up to devour her dishes, while women huddle together to analyze the ingredients in her dishes. Grandma glows in the praise and willingly shares recipe secrets. Spilled barbecue sauce in the oven gives birth to her unique smoke-flavored dinner rolls. An unintended spoonful of jelly rallies to become her unknown ingredient in her cookies. Her carelessness and creativity flow together in the creation of her own distinguished cooking method.

While grandma's cooking distinguishes her in her church, her general approach to cleaning distinguishes her within the family. The mundane task of cleaning the kitchen remains a shadowy concept just slightly beyond grandma's level of awareness. As a result, we are familiar with the concept of a chaotic kitchen, and we know the kitchen drill. Dump the dirty dishes out of the sink. This task requires finding some place to put the dirty dishes, a challenge to say the least. Dishes fill every available surface in the kitchen. They are propped precariously around the counter top and spill off the top of the linoleum table. There is only one solution to the problem: dump the dirty dishes out of the sink and onto the floor.

We pause briefly for a minor skirmish after we empty the sink. Everyone wants to wash dishes and no one wants to dry, a delusional moment for all of us because there will be plenty of dishes for everyone to have a turn washing and drying dishes. The skirmish ends when dad commandeers the sink.

The singing begins.

With dad at the helm of the sink, clean dishes churn quickly out of the water. Dad's efficiency creates another problem. Dishes still litter the counter top, leaving us no where to stack clean dishes. Well, if it worked once, why not try it again? We dump more dirty dishes onto the floor. Dad continues to churn through dirty dishes. We rinse, stack, and dry.

Singing continues.

Armed with clean dishes, we swing open the cabinet door. Spiraling stacks of dirty dishes sit snidely in the cabinets. By this time, we have accepted that the floor really is a counter top, and we dump more dirty dishes onto the floor. With the cabinet doors swung wide open, we scrub the shelves. Finally, some clean dishes come home to their rightful place in a cabinet.

Dad surrenders the sink to a child. We all exchange assignments: giving up drying dishes for rinsing dishes; rinsing dishes for washing dishes; and washing dishes for the dreaded drying of dishes. There is some justice in the world if dad ultimately has to dry dishes, right?

The singing continues.

Dishes on the floor disappear first, followed by dishes off the counter top. Once the counter top is cleared off, we have a few moments of wild adventure. Dad assigns each of us certain kitchen cabinets. Our mission is to find wayward concealed dirty dishes. Each of us has our personal pride at stake. No one wants to find something less interesting than our siblings. We pour ourselves into our investigations. The treasures are numerous—a bowl dotted with dried oatmeal, spoons laced with aged jelly, a large pan draped in dried barbecue sauce, a glass filled with soured milk, even a green bowl crusted with bread dough.

With treasures safely stowed in the sink, each of us returns to scrub the interior and exterior of each cabinet. Once cabinet sanctuary is established, we return to our ritual of washing dishes.

The singing continues.

Clean dishes fill the cabinets.

Our focus turns to the linoleum table still bowed with the humility of stacks of dirty dishes. At this point we are seasoned pros in the world of kitchen chaos. Without direction or instruction we fall into an orderly rhythm as we remove the dishes from the table and douse the table with soap and warm water.

The singing continues.

We are reaching the end of our quest. Two hurdles remain—the refrigerator and the stove. We flock toward the stove optimistically hoping to avoid the refrigerator. Luck is not on my side. While my younger brother and sister pull dirty dishes from the stove, my older sister and I tackle the carnage of the refrigerator.

If grandma had been conducting a scientific experiment in that refrigerator, she would have won a Pulitzer Prize for most outstanding moldy food. Regrettably, there is no such Pulitzer Prize. In his great wisdom, dad recognizes that the contaminants in the refrigerator are reaching a toxic level. Any container purchased with food in it is sentenced to immediate disposal. As a result, most of the contents of the refrigerator end up in the trash. We have to scrape food off of only a few plates, bowls, and pans.

The singing continues.

As the last dishes arise clean from soapy water, we recognize that our mission is complete.

Blue skies and rainbows and sunbeams from heaven . . .
The water drains from the sink.

Are what I can see when my Lord is living in me . . .
The dishtowels march to the dirty clothes hamper.

I know that Jesus is well and alive today . . .
One by one, we file out of the kitchen.

He makes his home in my heart . . .
Amazing what we can accomplish when we work together.

Never more will I be all alone . . .

Years later, the singing continues.

Since he promised me that we never would part.

the peanut butter

What draws families together is work and play. A common project, everyone involved, all working (or playing) to a common end. Whether washing dishes, scrubbing floors, or mowing the grass, shared activities provide an opportunity to create bonds and memories together. Doing dishes in grandma's kitchen gave us an opportunity to work together. Funny, years later, I remember the singing, not the sweating in a hot kitchen.

Doing the dishes gave us kids a chance to help out during a family crisis. Having a job to do made us important members of the family. There is never a more helpless feeling than having a loved one sick or injured, and there is nothing we can do. Their care is in the hands of doctors, nurses, and skilled professionals trained to take care of medical crises and emergencies. Although granddad didn't need our help, grandma needed our help. By pitching in together to clean the kitchen, we were contributing to the family and helping my grandparents.

Although we may be tempted to try to shield our children from the realities of taking care of aging parents, we may actually be depriving them of an opportunity to feel like an important contributing member of the family. We want to encourage our children to serve others as though they are serving God (1 Pet. 1:6-7) and to know that they can find strength from God to deal with difficult situations (Phil. 4:13).

Rather than sit idly and helplessly, we banded together, a family that loved each other: grandma and granddad, mom and dad, brothers and sisters. Our love forged a union that made it only natural for us to work together, pray together, and sing together as we made things better for those we loved.

–ADAPTED FROM
RANDALL MORRIS

the jelly

1. When we are faced with the physical needs of aging parents, we frequently want to protect our children from the challenges of caring for our parents. What are we trying to protect our children from?

2. The Bible calls us to "work with all our heart as though working for the Lord, not men" (Col. 3:23). How do we teach this value to our children while we are caring for our parents?

3. Describe ways you model serving others (1 Pet. 1:6-7) for your children.

4. Caring for aging parents can be an exhausting task. What can we do to keep our focus on Philippians 4:13?

the bread

Whatever you do,
work at it with all your heart,
as working for the Lord,
not for men,
since you know that you will
receive an inheritance
from the Lord as a reward.
It is the Lord Christ
you are serving.

–COLOSSIANS 3:23-24

No kind action ever stops with itself.

One kind action leads to another.

Good example is followed.

A single act of kindness throws out roots

in all directions,

and the roots spring up

and make new trees.

The greatest work that

kindness does to others is

that it makes them

kind themselves.

–Amelia Earhart

Bear in mind that

the wonderful things

you learn in your schools are the work

of many generations.

All this is put in your hands

as your inheritance in order that you may

receive it,

honor it,

add to it,

and one day faithfully hand it on to your children.

–Albert Einstein

3 the
reading
room

Some day you will be old enough
to start reading fairy tales again.

–C.S. Lewis

*T*he sun pushes through a dust-coated window. The smell of aged, musty books permeates the cubbyhole. A bed pushes back against one corner, leaving just enough space to maneuver through the room. Granddad's mussed gray hair flies in all directions. Wrinkles splinter through the rough stubble on his face. Bushy brows hood his eyes as he frowns in concentration. His shirt winds around his torso holding him captive. His aged body stretches the length of the bed with a book prompted up in front of him.

A maze of boxes and books form a fortress around the bed. Granddad has secured himself in the one corner of the house where grandma cannot reach him. Granddad spent his life as an electrician and can still meander through the maze of objects on the floor. However, grandma's rounded body isn't nimble. Grandma's feet shuffle through the house and find the maze too daunting to attempt.

Yet I am young and unafraid. I bulldoze through boxes and books and crawl up next to granddad. I snuggle next to his shoulder and inhale the distinct odor of Mentholatum and men's cologne that is granddad's smell. Granddad's eyes shift away from the book, and his bushy eyebrows tighten as he frowns distractedly.

"Read to me," I murmur.

Granddad's eyes focus on his book again, and his voice gently recites words I don't recognize and don't understand. The gentle sound of his voice comforts me. I snuggle closer. Granddad's voice murmurs on . . .

. . . Stolen moments lived in the secret world of words

. . . Solitude shared in the reading room.

Time tumbles forward.

Granddad's hair is thinner and his wrinkles are etched a little deeper across his face. His aging body stretches the length of the bed with a book prompted up in front of him. My legs are longer. I no longer bulldoze through the boxes and books. Instead I pick my way through boxes and books and crawl up next to granddad. Granddad's eyes drift away from the book, and he smiles slightly.

"Read to me," I murmur.

Granddad's smile widens, and he nods his head.

"You can read. Pick your own book."

Granddad pretends to focus his eyes on his book, but sneaks an occasional glance at me. My eyes scan the reading room. Books encase the room from wall to wall. Ancient bookcases sigh under the strain of the peculiar ordered disarray of books. A single row of books lines up neatly while snuggling into the recesses of each shelf. Other books turn at every angle along the edges of the shelves. A few scattered books perch on top of the rows.

Book subjects compete for the reader's attention. Books on radio repair, electricity, home improvement, history, and religion vie for shelf space. Bibles and Biblical commentaries confiscate a significant amount of space. In a secluded corner, *Reader's Digest Condensed Books* huddle on a shelf. I lift one of these books off the shelf. Although I only understand a small portion of what I read in a *Reader's Digest Condensed Book,* I don't understand anything I read in the other books.

I clamber back over beside granddad and pull a pillow up as close to him as I can. I snuggle my shoulder tightly against his shoulder. The familiar comforting smell of Mentholatum and cologne shrouds granddad. I open my book and prop it open like granddad and begin reading. I listen to his raspy breathing and read until my eyes grow heavy. Sleep overtakes me . . .

. . . Stolen moments lived in the secret world of words.

. . . Solitude shared in the reading room.

Time tumbles forward.

Granddad's hair is wispy and unkempt. His bushy brows and wrinkles create their own map across his face. Granddad's body stretches the length of the bed with a book propped up in front of him. My legs easily step over and around the boxes and books. I climb up on the bed and stretch out next to granddad.

Granddad looks up at me and asks, "What are you reading?"

I proudly present a *Hardy Boys Mystery* novel. Granddad nods and returns to his reading.

A small distance separates me from granddad while we read. I'm too old to snuggle up next to him, but I edge over as close as I can without actually snuggling up next to him. Comfort cloaks me as the familiar smells of Mentholatum and cologne assail my senses. I open my book and begin reading while the steady rhythm of granddad's raspy breathing reminds me of his presence. We both read until grandma calls us to dinner . . .

. . . Stolen moments lived in the secret world of words.

. . . Solitude shared in the reading room.

Time tumbles forward.

Granddad's stroke disassembles our reading room. A stranger buys the bed at a yard sale. Some of the Bibles and Biblical commentaries find new homes in the libraries of my uncles who are ministers. The books on electronics, home improvement, photography, and radio repair exit at the garage sale or are abandoned at a Goodwill store. I lay claim to a shelf full of Readers Digest Condensed Books. The books migrate to the shelves in my bedroom. When I am particularly sad about the loss of the reading room, my hands wander over the spines of the books. The contact with the books fills me with an odd combination of sadness and comfort. I mourn the loss of

. . . Stolen moments lived in the secret world of words.

. . . Solitude shared in the reading room.

Time tumbles forward.

Wednesday afternoon. Dread sneaks up my spine during the day. It is my turn to stay with granddad while mom takes grandma to shop for groceries. I only grudgingly agree to take care of granddad. I resent that the stroke has changed him. I don't want to be around him any more. Yet guilt propels me to stay with him. Both of my parents are doing everything they can to try to provide for my grandparents. I feel petty and small for even resenting having to take care of granddad, but it is how I feel.

The man lying in the hospital bed in my grandparents' house isn't my granddad. He can't hold a book. He can't read. His words slur together. His eyes stare vacantly into space. His body doesn't stretch out on the bed; it lies limp and dormant in the bed. The smell of antiseptic, urine, and bleach offend me, but I sit slumped in a bedside chair reading my history homework silently.

Granddad's eyes are closed. He is asleep. I'm not concentrating on reading my history. I'm thinking how relieved I am that I won't have to talk to granddad. What can I say to him? By suffering a stroke, granddad has betrayed me and abandoned me. Anger and sadness forge a wall around me.

Granddad stirs in his bed and mumbles. I lay down my textbook and stand to check on granddad. Truth be told, I am a little scared when I take care of my granddad. What if something happens? Will I know what to do? What if he dies while I'm with him? The very thought that he might die on my watch keeps me on edge. The mumbling continues for a few more minutes before granddad's words form.

"What . . . are . . . you . . . reading?" asks granddad in a raspy weak voice.

I begin explaining my history homework. Granddad's eyes grow clearer. When I finish my discourse on my history homework, I pause because I don't know what else to say.

"I . . . remember . . . my . . . homework," granddad pauses for a minute and seems to be searching for what to say next.

Then granddad begins in a halting voice, "Twenty froggies . . . went to school . . . down beside . . . a rushy pool."

Granddad begins to smile as he continues, "Twenty little coats of green . . . Twenty vests all white and clean." I think that the stroke has affected granddad and that he is spouting nonsense.

Granddad's voice grows stronger and clearer as he recites,

> *"We must be on time," said they,*
> *"First we study, then we play.*
> *That is how we keep the rule,*
> *When we froggies go to school."*

The singsong lilt of a child's voice carries on:

> *Master Bullfrog, brave and stern,*
> *Called the classes in their turn.*
> *Taught them how to nobly strive,*
> *Likewise how to leap and dive.*

I finally realize that granddad is reciting a poem he must have memorized in grade school. Granddad's voice carries on confidently,

> *From his seat upon a log,*
> *Taught them how to say, "Ker-Chog"*
> *Also how to dodge the blow*
> *From the sticks that bad boys throw.*
> *Twenty froggies grew up fast,*
> *Bullfrogs they became at last.*
> *Not one dunce among the lot,*
> *Not one lesson they forgot.*

With no hesitation, granddad continues on,

Polished in a high degree,
As each froggie ought to be.
Now they sit on other logs,
Teaching other little frogs.

Granddad stops his recitation, then asks, "Did I get an "A" on that one?"

"You sure did, Granddad," I respond. For a moment, my granddad is back. We are sharing our own special world of reading and learning. I reach out and gently squeeze his hand. I sit back down in my chair, open my history book, and begin reading to granddad...

. . . Stolen moments lived in the secret world of words.

. . . Solitude shared in the reading room.

Time tumbles forward.

The sun pushes through the window. The smell of cinnamon and chocolate permeates the cubbyhole. A desk pushes back against one corner leaving just enough space to maneuver through the room. Books encase the room from wall to wall. Modern bookcases display the peculiar ordered disarray of books. A single row of books line up neatly, while snuggling into the recesses of each shelf. Other books turn at every angle along the edges of the shelves. A few scattered books perch on top of the rows.

Book subjects compete for the reader's attention. Books on development, counseling, parenting, psychology, and religion vie for shelf space. Bibles and Biblical commentaries confiscate space.

To an outsider, it looks like an office.

To me, it is a reminder of . . .

. . . Stolen moments lived in the secret world of words.

. . . Solitude shared in the reading room.

the peanut butter

Reading develops imagination. Poems, novels, and short stories are entertaining and quickly become a part of the fabric of our lives. When we read we have to visualize and memorize what has been described. It transports us into the world of the author and his characters. Nothing is visually laid out for us. We have the freedom to shape and form much of what we read into our own images.

Certainly, sharing the reading room with granddad created a love of reading, but it also created a bond with my granddad that made the lessons he taught me after the stroke more meaningful. Granddad spent a life in Christian service and was compassionate with those around him. Although granddad taught me many lessons before his stroke, none of those lessons are as powerful as the lessons granddad taught me after the stroke.

Listening to granddad recite that childhood poem taught me about compassion and patience in dealing with others. Granddad lived out the Biblical admonish to "be careful, and watch yourselves closely so that you do not forget the things your eyes have seen or let them slip from your heart as long as you live. Teach them to your children and to their children after them." Deuteronomy 4:9-10. Granddad's frailty and vulnerability were tools to teach one of the greatest lessons of his life.

–ADAPTED FROM RANDALL MORRIS

the jelly

1. The activity I remember sharing with my granddad was reading. What activity do you remember sharing with your parents or grandparents? Why are the memories of these shared activities important to you?

2. In Deuteronomy 11:18-19, it says, "Fix these words of mine in your hearts and minds; tie them as symbols on your hands and bind them on your foreheads. Teach them to your children, talking about them when you sit at home and when you walk along the road, when you lie down and when you get up." When you shared time with your parents or grandparents, what did you learn about God's word?

3. When you share time with your children or grandchildren, what do you want to teach them about God's word?

4. Deuteronomy 4:9 states "Be careful, and watch yourselves closely so that you do not forget the things your eyes have seen or let them slip from your heart as long as you live. Teach them to your children and to their children after them." What do you need to watch yourself so that you do not let God's teachings slip from your heart?

the bread

Teach a child in the way he should go,
and when he is old he will not turn from it.

–PROVERBS 22:6

*Anyone who keeps the ability
to see beauty never grows old.*

–Franz Kafka

4

trashed
treasures

There are no rules

of architecture

for a castle

in the clouds.

–Gilbert K. Chesterton

Black trash bags dangle over the
edges of the Dumpster.

Discarded newspapers and books
beckon the reader.

Wine bottles and beer bottles
battle for rehabilitation.

Outgrown and battered clothing
grasps the hand of a quilter.

Broken radios and malfunctioning lamps
limp toward the electrician.

The procession in the Dumpster reaches
its climax today—garbage collection day.

Grandma recognizes the unique opportunities of a garbage collection day and rises early. Before the sanitation trucks rumble through the alleyways, grandma shuffles out the door wearing a worn pair of house shoes. Her shoulders slump forward as if her rounded body pulls them toward the earth. A housecoat flowered with pinks and yellows drapes over her hunched shoulders. The sheer turquoise fabric of her nightgown falls below the hem of her housecoat. A wig sits proudly on top of her wispy hair apparently unaware that it is turned askew.

Grandma can't be bothered with the details of getting dressed for the day. She shuffles down a practiced and prioritized path. Her mission is not depositing trash into a Dumpster. She is retrieving trash from several Dumpsters. I scramble to keep up with her.

Grandma ambles across her yard and toward the first Dumpster. I'm a novice at Dumpster diving, so grandma patiently explains to me how she prioritizes her route. She hits the "best" Dumpsters first. The "best" Dumpsters are the Dumpsters of neighbors who discard the trash with the most potential for rehabilitation.

She stops at the first Dumpster and reaches in with her bare hands and sorts through the contents. I cringe as I watch her hands emerge in unidentifiable gunk as they search for treasures. She gathers up a discarded pair of shoes, a tattered purse, and a broken lamp. She seems a little discouraged that she hasn't found more.

Grandma sighs and moves on to the next Dumpster. She pulls out some discarded bottles reeking of alcohol, but grandma doesn't seem to notice the odor. She progresses through the alley checking other Dumpsters. She adds tattered books and discarded clothes to her finds. I'm trailing behind her, dragging her treasure with me.

While grandma clambers round inside the Dumpsters, I am on the look out. I scan the alley in both directions, trying to detect if anyone is seeing us. I can't believe she is actually taking other people's possessions.

"Grandma, is it okay for you to do that?" I finally ask.

I'm hoping that my question will remind grandma that she shouldn't be looting other people's Dumpsters. I'm surprised at her response.

"People have thrown it away. Anybody can take it," grandma responds.

Grandma's Dumpster diving doesn't fit with what my parents have taught me. My parents have explained to me several times that it is wrong to take someone else's possessions without permission. Yet grandma says if someone has thrown it away, then we can take it without asking permission. I'm still a little skeptical, but as we rifle through Dumpsters down the alleyway without any consequences, I begin to believe my grandma. If someone else throws it away, then it is okay to take it.

When neither one of us can juggle an additional piece of trashed treasure, we return to grandma's house and unload grandma's treasures on her front porch. Once we unload our trashed treasures, we return to the regular route. Grandma knows which Dumpsters require a great deal of attention and which ones just a cursory glance. We continue to scavenge through Dumpsters in search of useful materials. By this time, I am fully engrossed in the adventure. My hands immerse themselves in refuse. I scavenge through Dumpsters searching for any treasure that will earn a word of praise from my grandma.

Later in the morning, I ask grandma another question.

"Why do you want other people's trash?"

"Sometimes people think they are throwing away trash when they are throwing away treasures."

I accept grandma's answer.

Grandma sees treasures where others see trash.

After spending most of the morning scavenging through Dumpsters, the rumble of the sanitation truck summons the end of the adventure. Grandma declares our Dumpster diving done for the day. We deposit the last of our treasures on grandma's front porch.

The second part of the adventure begins. Grandma sorts her treasures. The clothes are put aside to be used in quilting. I rinse the bottles off and line them up to dry along the sidewalk. Grandma cleans the shoes and purse and disappears into the house to stash them in her closet with her other clothes.

Grandma returns and surveys our finds with satisfaction. She disappears into the house, this time to retrieve granddad. Granddad enters the front porch. He doesn't seem nearly as excited as grandma about the finds, but when grandma asks him if he can fix the lamp; he dutifully picks it up. He turns it several directions, then mumbles that he thinks he can fix it. Once granddad has committed to fixing the lamp, grandma offers him the books she found. Granddad's eyes light up, and he disappears back into the house to examine the books.

After granddad leaves, I look around the enclosed front porch. Trashed treasures tumble in every available space on the front porch. Retrieving an item from one end of the porch requires excellent balance and agility because no walkway exists. Admittedly, refined treasures frequently emerge out of this chaos. Granddad and grandma transform the wine bottles and beer bottles into household decorations. Granddad takes old cigar boxes and shells and creates decorative carriages. Grandma engineers discarded clothing into creative quilts.

Grandma sees treasures where others see trash.

As I get older, I recognize that my grandma's behavior is out of the ordinary. Once I recognize how unusual Dumpster diving is, my mom explains to me that my grandparents lived through the Depression. Mom explains how grandma and granddad struggled to feed and clothe themselves and their kids during the Depression. As a result of that experience, grandma doesn't trust that she will have what she needs. She hoards discards as a way of feeling more secure. Grandma's house stays stacked with her trashed treasures.

When my grandparents move to Stinnett, much of my grandma's collection of trashed treasures is discarded again. Grandma has little opportunity to return to her Dumpster diving after the move. Her time is absorbed in caring for granddad. Occasionally, grandma ventures down the alley, but she limits her expeditions to a few Dumpsters in her block. When neighbors see grandma wandering down the alley, climbing in and out of Dumpsters, they assume that grandma is confused and lost. Neighbors usher grandma back down the alley to her house or call my mom to retrieve grandma. I know that grandma isn't lost or confused.

Grandma is on a great treasure hunt.

The lure of the overflowing Dumpster demands grandma's attention. She can't refuse the call to transform someone else's trash into a treasure. She still slips out the backyard and finds familiar sights.

Black trash bags dangle over the
edges of the Dumpster.

Discarded newspapers and books
beckon the reader.

Wine bottles and beer bottles
battle for rehabilitation.

Outgrown and battered clothing
grasps the hand of a quilter.

Broken radios and malfunctioning lamps
limp toward the electrician.

Now that I'm grown, I see "treasures" all around me. The procession in the Dumpster parades on through my life. I remember the lessons of seeing the broken and the discarded in a different way. I don't go Dumpster diving, but I try to see life through grandma's eyes.

I try to see value in the lives
of everyone I come in contact with.
I try to see past brokenness
in the lives of discarded people.
I try to see treasures.
I try to see what grandma saw.

the peanut butter

It takes a special kind of insight to see potential in what others have discarded, become disillusioned with, or lost interest in. Barnabas had this kind of insight to see the potential Paul didn't see in John Mark. Paul and Barnabas went on the first missionary journey, taking John Mark along with them. For some unexplained reason, John Mark left them early in their journey and returned to Jerusalem (Acts 13-14).

Later as Paul and Barnabas prepared to return to the cities and encourage the brethren of the first missionary journey, it was suggested that John Mark go with them. Paul was adamantly opposed. John Mark had not been with them on the first journey and Paul believed John Mark had no vested interest in the welfare of the churches they would be visiting. Perhaps Paul was wondering if John Mark could be trusted to finish the work on this journey after abandoning them on the first journey. Paul discarded John Mark; he was done with him (Acts 15:36-38).

As a result of Paul's unwillingness to work with John Mark, a sharp contention arose between Paul and Barnabas. When Paul and Barnabas could not resolve their differences, they parted ways. Barnabas took John Mark with him and went to Cyprus. Paul took Silas and went to Syria and Cilicia. Be assured this split did not hurt the church, in fact it doubled the evangelistic efforts of these two great men of God (Acts 15:39-41).

Paul did not see in John Mark what Barnabas saw. Barnabas saw something redeemable in John Mark. John Mark was salvageable. As scripture records the events of John Mark's life, we learn that Barnabas' willingness to work with a discarded man paid huge dividends for the Lord's kingdom. Eventually, John Mark wrote the Gospel of Mark. As Paul's life was drawing to a close, he even acknowledges John Mark's contributions to the Kingdom when he writes in 2 Timothy 4:11, "Get Mark and bring him with you, because he is helpful to me in my ministry."

Barnabas was able to see past what Paul saw in John Mark and was able to get the most out of him when his usefulness seemed to be at its ebb. We all need to look beyond what humans see in other people and try to see what God sees in them. Seeing other people through the Father's eyes will allow them to flourish at times when their energy and commitment to God seems to be ebbing.

–ADAPTED FROM RANDALL MORRIS

the jelly

1. It does take a special kind of insight to see potential in what others have discarded, become disillusioned with, or lost interest in. What kind of things do you see value in that others have discarded?

2. What things have your parents or grandparents seen value in that you didn't see value in? Why do these things have value for your parents or grandparents?

3. What things do you hope your children learn to value that others may not value?

4. In Acts 13-15, when Paul discarded John Mark, Barnabas used him for his ministry. How did Barnabas' ability to see potential in John Mark impact the church of the first century?

the bread

Brothers, think of what you were
when you were called.
Not many of you were wise by human standards;
not many were influential;
not many were of noble birth.
But God chose the foolish things
of the world to shame the wise;
God chose the weak things of the world
to shame the strong.

–1 CORINTHIANS 1:26-28

She's got her father's eyes,

Her father's eyes;

Eyes that find the good in things,

When good is not around;

Eyes that find the source of help,

When help just can't be found;

Eyes full of compassion,

Seeing every pain;

Knowing what you're going through

And feeling it the same.

Just like my father's eyes . . .

–Gary Chapman

5

snow's
a comin'

That which we persist in doing

becomes easier–

not that the nature

of the task

has changed,

but our ability to do has increased.

–Ralph Waldo Emerson

Wind sweeps through the streets and curls around squarely laid out Ranch style houses in our neighborhood. The urgings of a developing winter storm prod our neighbors to stay huddle in the warmth of their houses. No one seems to notice the steady rhythm of ka-ching, pwfff, ka-ching, pwfff, ka-ching, pwfff echoes through the neighborhood. Silence greets the persistent intrusion.

I stand atop a roof in the dim light of a late West Texas afternoon. Pink and orange ribbons twine together in the western horizon and wave goodbye to the day as the sun says its last farewells. Well-worn, oversized insulated coveralls cover me from neck to toes. The sleeves and legs of the coveralls extend beyond my arms and legs and are rolled up. My feet emerge in tennis shoes and my hands hide in the warmth of worn leather work gloves.

My hands wrap around a metal grip of an airnailer.

My finger tightens quickly and pulls the trigger.
Ka-ching . . . pwfff . . .
My arms recoil in response to the driving nail.
My finger tightens quickly and pulls the trigger again.
Ka-ching . . . pwfff . . .

The monotonous movement of running the airnailer comforts me as the wind grips me with its icy fingers. I focus on the job at hand. Dad and my brother, Charles, slap a shingle on the roof, quickly align it, and nod. I step forward and sling the airnailer toward the shingle. The airnailer connects with the shingle.

My finger tightens quickly and pulls the trigger.
Ka-ching . . . pwfff . . .
My arms recoil in response to the driving nail.
My finger tightens quickly and pulls the trigger again.
Ka-ching . . . pwfff . . .

Dad and Charles slap another shingle on the roof, align it, and nod. I step forward and sling the airnailer toward the shingle. The airnailer connects with the shingle.

> *My finger tightens quickly and pulls the trigger.*
> *Ka-ching . . . pwfff . . .*
> *My arms recoil in response to the driving nail.*
> *My finger tightens quickly and pulls the trigger again.*
> *Ka-ching . . . pwfff . . .*

The steady rhythm of work and the urgency of a developing winter storm drive dad to complete the roof. Dad sweeps Charles and I into his urgent mission. Grandma and granddad need a house and the weather won't stop the progress. Today, as soon as we got home from school, dad was waiting for us to go to work on the roof. Within fifteen minutes of getting home, we were scrambling onto the roof to go to work.

Now, light from the west fades.

Dad seems to ratchet up the work pace as though defying the fading sun and challenging the end of day. Charles and I pick up our pace as well. Dad and Charles slap another shingle on the roof, align it, and nod. I step forward and sling the airnailer toward the shingle. The airnailer connects with the shingle.

> *My finger tightens quickly and pulls the trigger.*
> *Ka-ching . . . pwfff . . .*
> *My arms recoil in response to the driving nail.*
> *My finger tightens quickly and pulls the trigger again.*
> *Ka-ching . . . pwfff . . .*

We repeat the pattern again and again as the light disappears. Finally, dad says, "Time to stop. We've got to get home for supper and church."

Dad crawls down the ladder. Charles and I hand tools down to dad. Dad climbs back up the ladder and to help us stretch plastic over the exposed parts of the roof and lay bundles of shingles at the edge of the plastic to keep it in place. Dad surveys the roof one final time and urges us down the ladder. Charles and I trudge to the edge of the roof and crawl down the ladder. Exhaustion creeps into our muscles and bones, but we neither one complain. Both Charles and I understand that dad feels an urgency that is driven by the oncoming winter storm.

Once I get home, I stop in the garage to deposit my winter clothes. I strip out of the hat, gloves, shoes, coveralls, and two sweatshirts. I hang the coveralls and sweatshirts on a hook behind the garage door and lay my other clothes on the freezer in the garage. Under all the winter clothes, sweat pours through my hair and skin from the exertion of working with dad.

I step inside the house and immediately step into a bathroom. I stare at my image in the mirror and see matted hair spun out of control by the removal of my winter cap. My short hair is standing askew in multiple directions. I run my fingers through my uncontrollable hair in an effort to impose some semblance of order. I fail drastically. I sigh in resignation and turn my attention to washing my hands. I turn on the water and watch it flow over my hands. My hands feel like they are wrapped in lead as I reach for the soap and wash them off. I turn off the water and head to the table.

Dad and Charles have both beat me to the table. I look at both of them expecting, maybe even hoping, to see that they are as exhausted as I am. Dad seems unfazed by our frantic work. We all bow our heads to pray. I hear the words dad utters as though I am in another room. I watch the food pass me on the table. I scoop meat loaf, mashed potatoes, and green beans onto my plate and then pick up a dinner roll. The food is warm and comforting as it settles in my stomach. Although still exhausted, I feel nurtured by the warmth of food. My body sighs in relief, appreciative of the opportunity to rest.

Too quickly supper ends and I pull myself out of my chair. I seem to be functioning in a haze as I walk to my room and pick out clothes to wear to church. I discard my worn jeans, long-sleeved ratty T-shirt, and old tennis shoes. I take a quick shower and dry my hair. Then I quickly don newer jeans, a sweater, and new tennis shoes. Mom doesn't like for me to wear jeans to church on Wednesday night, but she has gradually grown to accept my casual attire for mid week services. As I walk back through the living room, mom seems to recognize my weariness and doesn't even mention that I am wearing jeans. My family loads into the car and heads to church.

I struggle to stay focused during my Wednesday night class. Two of my favorite ladies in the congregation teach the teenage girls. I generally love the class, but once again weariness envelops me while I sit in the class. I'm not hearing everything that gets said in class. Instead my head and heart are listening to a weary body plead for respite. When church ends, my family loads back into our brown Oldsmobile Bonneville and we drive the block back home.

As we drive home, dad is at the wheel of the car and says, "I'm going back over to mom and dad's house tonight. I'd like to get the rest of that roof on before the snow hits."

Mom's face signals how worried she is and she responds, "George, it's completely dark out on that roof, you can't possibly finish it tonight."

"I can hook up some flood lights and work until the snow starts."

Mom sighs as she recognizes that dad has made up his mind. "I don't want you up on the roof by yourself at night and it is too late for the kids to be working on a school night."

Before I recognize what I'm doing, I blurt out, "Mom, I can help Dad. It won't take that long to finish the roof."

Charles chimes in, "I'll help too. We don't have that much to finish."

Mom apparently thinks it is a better idea to have three of us on the roof, rather than dad being on the roof by himself. She acquiesces and issues a final warning, "George, I don't want those kids to miss school tomorrow."

Before dad can respond, Charles and I in unison assure mom, "I won't miss school tomorrow."

Once we reach the house, the entire disrobing process that took place before church reverses itself. I go to my bedroom and slip back into my worn jeans, long-sleeved ratty T-shirt, and old tennis shoes. My muscles protest against the simple effort of pulling on my clothes. My muscles are stiff as I walk back through the living room and bend down and hug mom as she sits in the recliner grading papers and assure her that we won't stay out too late.

Charles and I make our way to the garage and begin putting on our armor against the icy wind. We both pull on hooded sweatshirts, coveralls, gloves, and winter hats. My legs are tight and seem unwilling to follow my bidding to move as we troop back across the street to grandma and granddad's house. Dad is on the roof in the process of securing the floodlights when we arrive. As soon as dad has the floodlights in place, he climbs back down the ladder and sends us up the ladder with a wordless wave. With our muscles groaning and protesting, we climb back on the roof and haul tools back up as dad hands them to us from the ground.

The icy wind wails and whips against us as we position ourselves to begin laying shingles again. I question why I volunteered to be back on the roof when I could be home in bed. I think about the cozy warmth of being curled up in my bed wrapped in an electric blanket. I feel tears form at the corners of my eyes. The stinging wind quickly reminds me that crying won't improve the situation. A job must be finished. The snow won't wait until tomorrow.

Dad and Charles begin our routine. They slap a shingle on the roof, slowly align it, and nod. I step forward and sling the airnailer toward the shingle. The airnailer connects with the shingle.

My finger tightens quickly and pulls the trigger.
Ka-ching . . . pwfff . . .
My arms recoil in response to the driving nail.
My finger tightens quickly and pulls the trigger again.
Ka-ching . . . pwfff . . .

Dad and Charles slap another shingle on the roof, align it a little quicker, and nod. I step forward and sling the airnailer toward the shingle. The airnailer connects with the shingle.

My finger tightens quickly and pulls the trigger.
Ka-ching . . . pwfff . . .
My arms recoil in response to the driving nail.
My finger tightens quickly and pulls the trigger again.
Ka-ching . . . pwfff . . .

My muscles begin to warm up and the rhythm of the work begins to lull me back into a comforting routine. Dad and Charles slap another shingle on the roof, align it quickly, and nod. I step forward and sling the airnailer toward the shingle. The airnailer connects with the shingle.

My finger tightens quickly and pulls the trigger.
Ka-ching . . . pwfff . . .
My arms recoil in response to the driving nail.
My finger tightens quickly and pulls the trigger again.
Ka-ching . . . pwfff . . .

The wind whips a few snowflakes past us as we work quickly. The urgency of the job replaces thoughts of sleep and comfort. The snow's a comin' and the job has to be finished.

Wind sweeps through the streets and whips a few snowflakes past us as we work quickly. No one notices the steady rhythm of ka-ching, pwfff, ka-ching, pwfff, ka-ching, pwfff that echoes through the night and into the early morning. The steady rhythm of work continues until the last shingle is laid.

the peanut butter

The snowstorm created a sense of urgency to complete the roofing of the house, yet this important, urgent work stopped for Bible class. Weariness of body, coldness to the bone, the threat of the coming storm are not reasons to miss Bible class. Dad knew it was important that we "seek first God's Kingdom and his righteousness" (Matt. 6:33).

After Bible class was over dad knew that the work on the roof had to be finished. He didn't expect us to go back and help him work on the roof, but we knew that he needed help. We knew that we could help him complete the roof and we knew that he valued our help. Together we could get the job done and done right before the snowstorm hit.

As an adult I understand that my parents helped us recognize that we played an important role in our family and in the care of my grandparents. Through their examples they taught us compassion and a tremendous appreciation of a work ethic. Unfortunately, parents today often believe that their children deserve "to have it better" than they had it as children.

As a result of this belief system, parents eliminate the work expectations they have for their children. Children grow up waiting for "luck" or "good fortune" to come their way, and have no realization that in the absence of hard work, "luck" and "good fortune" are myths. All of our children deserve to have the opportunity to contribute through hard work to the family. Every child deserves to have the opportunity to learn "to do whatever your hand finds to do, for God is with you" (2 Sam. 10:7).

–ADAPTED FROM
RANDALL MORRIS

the jelly

1. When we are sandwiched taking care of our parents and our children, it is easy to forget how important it is to seek God first. What pulls your focus away from you relationship with God? What can you do to keep your focus on God?

2. Stopping in the middle of a pressing project or an urgent crisis to attend church or to attend to the needs of others sends a strong message of commitment to those around us. Try to recall an instance when your parents or grandparents interrupted a seemingly urgent situation to attend to something more important.

3. Providing care for our parents provides many opportunities to let our children learn the value of hard work and caring for others. How are you teaching your children about the value of hard work and caring for others?

4. Working together can strengthen bonds in a family and help children learn that they have important roles in a family. What roles do your children have in family? How do they believe they contribute to the family?

the bread

"Whatever your hand finds to do,
do it with all your might, for in the grave,
where you are going, there is neither working
nor planning nor knowledge nor wisdom."

–ECCLESIASTES 9:10

Loving a child doesn't mean giving in to all his whims; to love him is to bring out the best in him, to teach him to love what is difficult.

–Nadia Boulanger

6

taking
turns

If you want children to keep their feet on the ground, put some responsibility on their shoulders.

–Abigail Van Buren

*L*incoln logs scatter across the floor, a G. I. Joe Jeep scoots under the bed, and two sets of hands tug a G. I. Joe action figure. Bodies sway back and forth as each child pulls the G. I. Joe to try to wring it from the grasp of the other child.

"It's my turn."
"It's my turn."
"You all ready had a turn."
"You've had two turns."
"It's not fair. Give me my turn."

A mother's voice breaks through the rowdy disagreement of young children, "You two better find a way to play together. If I have to get involved, neither one of you will get another turn."

My brother, Charles, and I stop tugging the G. I. Joe action figure. Our hands fall to our sides and G. I. Joe falls to the floor. We glare at each other and turn away from one another and G. I. Joe. My hands begin stacking Lincoln logs and my brother pulls the Jeep from under the bed. The verbal jostling falls silent, but the underlying sibling rivalry simmers.

Three years later, a West Texas wind shoves a football off its intended path. The football hammers into the ground and rolls end over end in dry grass for several yards. Young feet in scuffed tennis shoes scurry toward the football. Feet stop and hands lunge for the football. The football tumbles and shoots out of the huddle of feet and hands. A scuffle for control of the ball begins because whoever controls the football gets to play quarterback.

"It's my turn."
"It's my turn."
"You all ready had a turn."
"You've had two turns."
"It's not fair. Give me my turn."

A mother's voice breaks through the rowdy disagreement of children, "You two better find a way to play together. If I have to get involved, neither one of you will get another turn."

Charles and I step away from the scuffling. Our hands fall to our sides and the football slowly turns end over end until it lies still. We glare at each other and turn away from one another. Each of us turns back toward our friends and let someone else take over the role of the quarterback. The verbal jostling falls silent, but the underlying sibling rivalry simmers.

Three years later, verbal jostling continues and sibling rivalry simmers, but childhood games consume less of our time. Since granddad's stroke, responsibilities have shifted. Every member of the family has adjusted. After school every day, mom goes to my grandparents' house to help them until suppertime. Since mom is helping my grandparents, each of us kids assumes additional chores. Mom develops a weekly schedule of chores. The weekly schedule of chores demands respect and compliance. Every one of us has a different responsibility on a different day. We have a day to clean bathrooms, a day to do the dishes after supper, a day to cook supper, and a day to do laundry.

If we miss our turn to do laundry, we have to wait until the next week to get another turn or negotiate with a sibling to gain access to the washer and dryer during someone else's laundry day. The negotiations are familiar.

"It's my turn," Charles states.

"I know it's your turn, but I missed my turn. I need to wash jeans," I respond.

"You should have thought of that when it was your day to do laundry. You've all ready had a turn this week. It's your problem if you didn't use your turn. You'll have to wait until next week" goads Charles.

"Come on, Charles. You've finished your laundry for the week. You don't need the rest of your turn. I've got to wash jeans. It's not fair that you won't share."

"Not my problem. You didn't do your laundry on your day. Why should I give you part of my day?"

"You're finished, just let me run a load or two. Okay?"

Charles shakes his head and denies my request.

"Okay, Fine. If you let me do my laundry today, I'll finish cleaning the bathroom for you."

"You'll finish cleaning the bathroom?"

"Yeah, I'll finish the bathroom."

"Okay, you can use the rest of my day, but you better clean the bathroom."

The verbal jostling of the negotiations falls silent, but the underlying sibling rivalry simmers. No need for a mother's voice to negotiate the disagreement of children. We have reluctantly found ways to work together and make sure everyone gets a turn.

Of course, there is one exception to these negotiated sibling truces—cooking supper. Each of us is an inexperienced cook, but Charles develops the most creative culinary skills. He takes pride in creating peanut butter, mustard, and pickle sandwiches. I try to tolerate his creativity because if I complain about his cooking I'll have to take his turn and mine turn next week. I don't want an extra turn.

One evening, my family sits down to the table. In surveying the table, I see only one dish. In the center of the table sits a white bowl with cubes of red and green Jell-O. I look around expecting to see more food waiting to be served. I scan the stove and countertop in the kitchen. Nothing.

"Where's the rest of supper?" I ask.

"This is supper," Charles responds.

"This isn't supper. This is Jell-O."

"It's my turn to cook and I wanted Jell-O for supper."

"It may be your turn to cook, but Jell-O is not supper."

"It is if it's my turn to cook."

"It's not fair for you to fix only Jell-O for supper."

A mother's voice breaks through a rowdy disagreement. "Beth, since you don't like what Charles cooked for supper, you can take his turn and your turn next week."

The verbal jostling falls silent, but the underlying sibling rivalry simmers. A mother's voice has negotiated the disagreement. Charles sits smiling triumphantly in victory, while I sit pouting in defeat. After years of negotiations, he has finally outwitted me with Jell-O of all things. He managed to get mom to intervene. I don't like the results.

Years later. The phone rings. Mom's shaking voice tells me that dad has fallen and is being transported by ambulance to the hospital in Amarillo. I meet the ambulance at the hospital. I don't even get a glimpse of my dad before he is moved from the emergency room to surgery. He has fallen from a ladder while he was inspecting a roof at work.

The ladder came out from under him and he hit the concrete feet first shattering most of his lower extremities. Dad's ankle is reconstructed in surgery. He has broken both of his legs in multiple places, cracked his elbow, and cracked some ribs. He spends several days in intensive care. As a family, we develop a regular routine of visits between work, school, and other commitments. When dad is moved from ICU to a hospital room, we know he will need someone to stay with him. Of course, patterns established years ago continue.

"I'll take the first turn," I volunteer.
"I'll take the first turn," my brother responds.
"You need to get your rest, you have too many things going on."
"You need your rest too. You are in the middle of a school year."
"I don't mind taking the first turn."
"I don't mind either."
"Are you sure? I'll take the first turn."
"I'm sure. You can have the next turn."
"Thanks. I'm going to get some rest."
"I'll see you for the next shift."

I turn and leave the sterile hospital room. Charles settles into the chair beside dad's bed. I remember a mother's voice prompting us, "You two better find a way to play together. If I have to get involved, neither one of you will get another turn." I'm not sure we ever learned how to play together, but we have learned how to work together. The verbal jostling falls silent. The sibling rivalry ceases to simmer.

Both of us will have our turn.

the peanut butter

Jesus said it is more blessed to give than to receive (Acts 20:35), but giving is not a natural act. Parents who are intent on teaching their children to love the Lord (Eph. 6:4) must be uncompromising in their demand that their children learn to respect each other and give to one another.

Sometimes this requires direct intervention, and other times just the threat of intervention is sufficient. What must be understood is that sibling rivalries do exist (Gen. 37:4), but they must not be allowed to destroy the home and the family or its peace and harmony (Gen. 37:19-22).

My brother and I had our rivalries, but we also understood that our disputes would be allowed only for a limited amount of time (Eph. 4:26) before they had to be resolved, either by silent simmering, or finding true, negotiated settlements where both sides got something of benefit out of the deal.

Above all our rivalries were not allowed to disrupt our home. In work or play, throughout childhood and into adulthood those who cannot negotiate a satisfactory settlement are the ones who never learned to gracefully withdraw from a dispute before it becomes destructive (Matt. 5:25). Functioning citizens, families, and church workers have learned to differentiate between what is petty and requires silent resolution through abandonment; what is worthy of negotiated settlement; and what cannot be compromised but must be defended and protected at all costs.

My parents taught us a priceless lesson that continues to play out into adulthood. Although Charles and I were rivals as children, we have become close friends as adults. I don't know what I would do without my brother and sisters when faced with a crisis in adulthood. Our squabbles in adulthood are no longer about getting our own way; instead they are about our genuine concern for one another.

–ADAPTED FROM RANDALL MORRIS

the jelly

1. Most siblings have rivalries. What do you remember sibling rivalries being centered on in your home?

2. Have your sibling rivalries carried over into adulthood? Why or why not?

3. How do you think your relationships with your siblings are impacting how you are caring for your parents or grandparents?

4. What do you hope your children's relationships with their siblings will be like when they are adults? What are you doing to help them develop their sibling relationships?

the bread

*Love the Lord your God
with all your heart and with all your soul
and with all your strength and with all your mind;
and, love your neighbor as yourself.*

–LUKE 10:27

A sister is a little bit

of childhood that can never be lost.

–Marion C. Garretty

I do not believe that the accident of birth makes people sisters and brothers. It makes them siblings. Gives them mutuality of parentage. Sisterhood and brotherhood are conditions people have to work at. It's a serious matter. You compromise, you give, you take, you stand firm, and you're relentless . . . and it is an investment.

–Maya Angelou

7

rub-a-dub-dub

Speak tenderly to them.

Let there be kindness in your face, in your eyes,

in your smile, in the warmth of your greeting.

Always have a cheerful smile. Don't only give

your care, but give your heart as well.

–Mother Teresa

*S*upper ends. The routine begins. Mom picks me up off the chair and sets me firmly on my feet.

"Time for your bath," she prompts.

I protest. Shaking my head from side to side, I wail, "I don't want to take a bath."

"I know you don't want to take a bath, but you'll feel better after a bath."

Mom firmly takes my hand and leads me to the bathroom. Once in the bathroom, she turns on the water in the bathtub and has me lie down on the bathroom floor so she can undress me. She carefully unbuttons my shirt and slips my arms out of the sleeves before pulling the shirt over my head. She then unsnaps and unzips my pants and wriggles the pants down off of my legs. When all my clothes are removed, she puts both hands under my arms and gently lifts me into the bath water.

Mom dips the soap into the water and begins to lather my arms with soap. She works from the tips of my fingers to my elbows to my shoulders. She uses a soothing circular motion as she works. She scrubs my back and stops to tickle me a few times. All the time she works she hums a little to herself and occasionally sings:

> *"Rub-a-dub-dub*
> *Three men in a tub,*
> *And who do you think they be?*
> *The butcher, the baker, the candlestick maker,*
> *All as clean as they can be . . ."*

Mom works the soap across my legs, stopping to tickle my toes, then scrubs vigorously at my knees. Then mom reaches for a wash cloth and dips it in water to begin rinsing the soap off. The water trickles across my limbs and torso in a soothing river. Mom continues to hum as she works. Once all the soap has been washed away, mom reaches for a washcloth and the shampoo. All the time she works she hums a little to herself and occasionally sings:

"Rub-a-dub-dub
Three men in a tub,
And who do you think they be?
The butcher, the baker, the candlestick maker,
All as clean as they can be . . ."

A break in the music.
"Time to do your hair."

Mom dips the washcloth in water again and lets the water from the washcloth pour through my hair. She wipes the water from my face before pouring shampoo into her hand. She rubs both hands together and then spreads the shampoo through my hair. Her fingertips massage my scalp while she works the shampoo through my hair. She eases my head back and the rinses my hair under the water faucet. Mom again wipes water from my face. All the time she works she hums a little to herself and occasionally sings:

"Rub-a-dub-dub
Three men in a tub,
And who do you think they be?
The butcher, the baker, the candlestick maker,
All as clean as they can be . . ."

A break in the music.
"Time to get out of the tub."

Mom puts both hands under my arms and lifts me out of the tub. She quickly wraps a towel around me and begins to dry my hair. Once she has toweled my hair dry, she begins to rub the towel vigorously along my torso and limbs to dry them as quickly as she can. Once mom is satisfied that I am dry enough, she lays the towel across my shoulders and reaches for the lotion. She pours lotion into her palm and rubs it between her hands. Once the lotion is warm, mom begins applying it to my arms, elbows, and shoulders. She works her way down my back, legs, knees, and finally to my feet. She has me sit down so she can put lotion on my feet. She spreads the lotion across both the tops and bottoms of my feet and then caresses the bottom of my feet with her thumbs. When mom finishes with the lotion, she folds the towel and hangs it up to dry.

She continues to hum.
"Time to get you dressed."

Mom holds my underwear out so I can step into it. She lets me hold onto her with one hand while I step into my underwear. Then mom holds out my pajama pants for me to step into. Once I step into my pajama pants, mom grabs both sides of the elastic at the waist and pulls them up. She reaches for my pajama top and pulls it over my head. She gently works my arms into the sleeve. She straightens my pajamas and gently smoothes my hair.

She reaches over and kisses my forehead and says, "Now, don't you feel better?"

More than a decade later. School ends. The afternoon routine begins.

Mom packs up her papers to grade at home and loads all of us kids into the car. When we get home, mom unloads her school work and changes clothes. She gives us a few words of prompting about chores, and then heads across the street to my grandparents' house.

Occasionally, I walk across the street with mom. Mom's job is to bathe my granddad, shave him, assist with his physical therapy, sit him up for awhile in the living room, and then help grandma fix supper. When I follow Mom to my grandparents' house, I stay in the living room while my mom bathes my granddad. I sit on my grandma's couch and try to watch reruns of the Brady Bunch on TV, but I can't drown out the sounds in the next room.

When mom enters granddad's room, she reminds him, "Time for your bath."

Granddad protests loudly, "I don't want to take a bath. Please don't make me take a bath."

Mom gently reassures granddad, "I know you don't want to take a bath, but you'll feel better after a bath."

I hear mom tell granddad, "You need to help me. I'm going to lift you into a sitting position.

Mom grunts as she lifts granddad into a sitting position. Granddad groans.

"Now, Dad, put your right foot under your left foot to help me swing your feet over the side of the bed."

Mom grunts as she maneuvers granddad to the edge of the bed. Granddad groans and cusses. I hear mom move the wheelchair close to the bed and lock the brakes.

"Okay, Dad, I'm going to stand you up and turn you around into the wheelchair."

The rhythm of grunts, groans, and cussing continues. I hear mom unlock the brakes on the wheelchair and wheel it out of granddad's room, down the hall, and into the bathroom. The sounds are more muffled, but still easily heard in the living room.

"Dad, I'm going to take off your pajamas and move you to the chair here in the shower." Grunts, groans, and cussing continue as mom removes granddad's pajamas and moves him to the shower chair. I block out the sounds by humming to myself a familiar tune:

"Rub-a-dub-dub
Three men in a tub,
And who do you think they be?
The butcher, the baker, the candlestick maker,
All as clean as they can be . . ."

I hear the water cascading in the shower. Granddad groans and cusses in aggravation. Mom's voice reassures him, "Dad, you need a bath, you'll feel better in a minute. I know you don't like to take a bath." My mom murmurs as she bathes granddad.

"Dad, I'm going to wash your arms."

The sounds of water continue.

"I'm washing your back now."

The humming in my head grows louder.
"I'm washing your legs, Dad."

The moans and cussing continue.
"Now, Dad, I'm going to wash your feet."

The familiar tune continues in my head.

> *"Rub-a-dub-dub*
> *Three men in a tub,*
> *And who do you think they be?*
> *The butcher, the baker, the candlestick maker,*
> *All as clean as they can be . . ."*

The sounds of the water fall silent.
"Dad, I'm going to dry you off and then we'll get some clean pajamas on you. You'll feel much better."

The unique mixture of grunts, groans, and cussing continue, until the sounds of the wheelchair coming down the hall signal the end of bath time. Mom pushes the wheelchair into the living room and locks the brakes. She puts both her hands under granddad's arms and lifts him from the wheelchair to the recliner. She tucks a blanket around his lap. Mom straightens granddad's pajamas and gently smoothes his hair.

She reaches over and kisses his forehead and says, "Now, don't you feel better?"

Nearly three decades later. Supper ends. The routine begins. I pick up a child and lift him out of his booster chair and set him firmly on his feet.

"Time for your bath," I prompt.

I take his hand and lead him to the bathroom. Once in the bathroom, I turn on the water in the bathtub and lay him on the rug in the bathroom to undress him. I carefully unbutton his shirt and slip his arms out of the sleeves before pulling the shirt over his head. I unsnap and unzip his jeans and wriggle them down off his legs. When all his clothes are removed, I put both hands under his arms and gently lift him into the bath water.

I dip the soap into the water and begin to lather his arms with soap. I work from the tips of his fingers to his elbows to his shoulders. I use a soothing circular motion as I work. I scrub his back and stop to tickle him a few times. All the time I work, I hum a little to myself and occasionally sing:

"Rub-a-dub-dub
Three men in a tub,
And who do you think they be?
The butcher, the baker, the candlestick maker,
All as clean as they can be."

the peanut butter

My mom's care of my granddad was a wonderful example of servitude. She clearly understood that following Jesus meant following his example. Jesus "did not come to be served, but to serve" (Matt. 20:28). His many miracles (John 2:11; 20:30-31), countless hours of teaching (Mark 6:34), innumerable miles traveled, and meals lost (Mark 3:20) were all sacrifices made for the salvation of man.

On the night of His betrayal He washed the feet of the disciples. Jesus exemplified that the most demeaning service expected of the lowest slave in the household: washing the feet of visitors in the home is not too small, unimportant, or demeaning for the disciples of Jesus Christ. Jesus reminds us, "Now that I, your Lord and Teacher, have washed your feet, you also should wash one another's feet. I have set you an example that you should do as I have done for you. I tell you the truth, no servant is greater than his master, nor is a messenger greater than the one who sent him. Now that you know these things, you will be blessed if you do them" (John 14:17).

Whatever my brother, sister, father, mother, son, daughter, child—even enemy (Rom. 12:19-21) needs, I am called to try to meet based upon Jesus' example.

No child relishes having to bathe a nearly invalid parent or to hear the cussing and groaning unleashed by the ravages of disease. Yet such an act certainly falls within the scope of the Master's example. "Let us not become weary in doing good, for at the proper time we will reap a harvest if we do not give up" (Gal. 6:9).

–ADAPTED FROM
RANDALL MORRIS

the jelly

1. Why is it difficult for us to become the caregivers for our parents?

2. What has been the most difficult task you have had to do in taking care of your parents or grandparents?

3. How would you feel about one of your children having to provide daily personal care for you?

4. How have you felt about providing daily personal care for your children when they were young? Do you believe that they could experience the same reactions to caring for you? Why or why not?

the bread

*Instead, whoever wants
to become great among you
must be your servant,
and whoever wants to be first
must be your slave—
just as the Son of Man
did not come to be served,
but to serve, and to give his life
as a ransom for many.*

–MATTHEW 20:26-28

Out of intense complexities,
intense simplicities emerge.

–Winston Churchill

8

pieces of
memories

Be a life long or short,

its completeness depends

on what it was lived for.

–David Starr Jordan

Color scraps of fabric overflow a box—

Remnants from a bright colored dress worn by a young lady, newly married on a summer evening—

The flowered pinks of a girl's dress worn on the first day of school—

Darker brown fabric from men's trousers worn to a business meeting that launched a career—

Sheets worn with the wear of a young child's tossing and turning in bed—

The black swatch of a garment worn to the funeral of a beloved friend—

A farmer's overalls streaked with the toil of labor and the grit of the earth—

The blue jumper of a baby's first Easter Sunday—

> Grandma's box of quilting scraps holds pieces of memories . . . memories of laughter and tears . . . memories of dreams found and dreams abandoned . . . memories of faith and disillusionment . . . memories of loved ones and strangers.

When grandma creates a new quilt, she blends the memories held in each fabric into a patchwork to hold new memories. Even the process of creating a new quilt is a process of making memories. When grandma begins to piece a new quilt, she launches into a well-rehearsed ritual. Initially grandma circles through her house pulling out boxes. Boxes emerge from under beds, from the hidden recesses of closets, and from behind furniture. With considerable effort, grandma unites the boxes in the living room. Each box creates its own maze of memories.

Grandma's forehead creases in concentration as her hands scavenge through the boxes, pulling out remnants of fabrics and patterns. She seems oblivious to anything except the fabrics in her hands. Occasionally, a look of astonishment emerges as she pulls out a quilt pattern to find a stitch or two of thread connecting it to a swatch of fabric.

There's no rhyme or reason to the way grandma stores her fabrics and patterns. Wherever something lands is where it stays buried until the next quilt excavation begins; yet she has an uncanny sense of where every fabric and pattern lands. The process of determining what resources are available is a great deal of the joy of the adventure.

Once grandma inventories the remnants and patterns, she begins the laborious process of deciding the design of the quilt. She shuffles back and forth between boxes lifting and sifting through fabrics and patterns. She bends over and sorts, then she sighs and straightens her back. Her hands rest on her hips for a few minutes before she submerges herself in the boxes again. She mutters softly while she works. Occasionally she stops, stands upright, and inspects a fabric or pattern. With a quick grunt, she tosses the pattern or fabric back into the box or toward the center of the living room floor.

After grandma picks her way through the maze of boxes several times, her hands deftly sort the fabrics on the living room into several piles. Patterns scatter across the piles of fabrics. Grandma reaches for scissors and begins shaping scraps of fabric into shapes for the quilt. Grandma's fingers nimbly hold patterns and fabrics together while her scissors expertly cut fabric without the restraint of pins. She carelessly drops fabric replicas of the pattern on the floor beside her chair. Frequently, she cuts fabrics without using a pattern. Her hands seem to memorize the shapes and patterns and instinctively know how to cut the fabric. My inexperienced hands struggle to sort fabrics then pin patterns onto those fabrics. I carefully trace the patterns with scissors as I try to emulate grandma. The pile beside grandma's chair easily eclipses my small stack of fabric.

Cutting the fabric for the quilt takes several days. Several days of sharing

. . . the frustration of failed stitches and patterns misplaced
. . . the success of well-placed stitches and blended colors
. . . tales of a life long lived and a life barely lived
. . . stories of foundational faith and fledgling faith.

Once the fabric is cut, grandma begins piecing the swatches together. She plucks various shapes and pieces of fabric out of the piles. She seems to know instinctively which pieces belong together. She uses solid black pieces repeatedly in the quilt to create focal points. She scatters greens and oranges in a random pattern throughout the blues and reds. She creates her own masterpiece with the pieces of memories.

Grandma hands me fabrics to stitch together. Grandma and I sew the smaller pieces of fabric together by hand. Grandma's stitches fall neatly in line at regular intervals. My stitches meander around the edges of the fabric. Grandma's blocks of quilt pieces lay neatly flat on her floor. My blocks of quilt pieces are distinguished by ridges and puckers representing stitches.

Piecing the blocks together takes several days. Several days of sharing

. . . the frustration of failed stitches and patterns misplaced
. . . the success of well-placed stitches and blended colors
. . . tales of a life long lived and a life barely lived
. . . stories of foundational faith and fledgling faith.

When all the blocks are pieced together, we retreat to grandma's back bedroom to work at the sewing machine. The sewing machine sits right under a north window. Light edges through the room. Grandma leans over my shoulder while I wrestle with blocks of fabric. The ragged-edged pieces surge under the sewing machine. The needle marches through the fabrics creating stitches to connect the blocks. When the sewing machine falls silent, the quilt top is complete.

We have created a new quilt. We have blended the memories held in each fabric into a patchwork to hold new memories. In the process of creating this quilt, grandma has helped me create new memories. The color scraps of fabric that once overflowed boxes have become memories of laughter and frustration shared with grandma in creating the quilt.

Grandma's new quilt holds pieces of our shared memories . . . memories of success and frustration . . . memories of laughter and tears . . . memories of dreams shared and sheltered by love . . . memories of grandma's aged faith and my fledgling faith . . . memories of time shared.

Grandma takes great pride in piecing a quilt for each of her grandchildren. I get the privilege of helping her piece several of those quilts. When the time comes to piece my quilt, grandma chooses her favorite pattern and pulls out a box of her best scraps. She has been putting back pieces of fabric for several years to save for my quilt. Grandma has saved the best for me. Yet I find myself drawn to a different box.

In a different box, the leftover blocks from my cousin's quilts huddle together in disarray. Each leftover block symbolizes a memory shared with grandma. Those leftover blocks shrouded in memories are the pieces I want in my quilt.

"Grandma, can't we use this for my quilt?" I ask expectantly.

"Those are scraps from other quilts," responds grandma.

"I know, Grandma. They are scraps from quilts we worked on together. Wouldn't it be fun to have a quilt made from the scraps of the other quilts?"

"Those scraps won't look right in a quilt. The blocks are different sizes and the fabrics are different colors. The quilt won't look good," protests grandma.

"Couldn't we do something to make it look right?" I plead.

Grandma reluctantly shrugs and begins to pull the leftover blocks out of the box. I watch as she sorts them one way and then another way. She creates stacks and rearranges them. Eventually the frown leaves her forehead and she begins to mutter to herself. Finally she stops the sorting and drops into a chair. She nods her assent.

Together we piece the quilt blocks together to create my quilt. The finished quilt contains remnants from all the quilts I've helped grandma piece as well as some quilts grandma pieced before she moved to Stinnett.

Grandma was right.
The muslin in the quilt blocks is different colors.
The blocks clearly are scraps from other quilts.
The colors in the quilt don't coordinate well.

Yet, I see something very different than what grandma sees. Those leftover quilt blocks aren't scraps—they are memories. The color scraps of fabric that once overflowed boxes have become memories of laughter and frustration shared with grandma in creating the quilt.

What once was a remnant from a bright-colored dress worn by a young lady, newly married on a summer evening, has become the piece in the quilt that I had to cut three different times because I couldn't get the pattern pinned on the fabric correctly.

What once was the flowered pinks of a girl's dress worn on the first day of school has become the swatch of pink I sewed onto the wrong block and had to rip apart twice.

What once was the darker brown fabric from men's trousers worn to a business meeting that launched a career has become the quilt block that got jammed in the sewing machine.

What once was a sheet worn with the wear of a young child's tossing and turning in bed has become the lining of quilt that I sewed into a wad.

What once was the black swatch of a garment worn to the funeral of a beloved friend has become the quilt piece I couldn't find because I was sitting on it.

What once was a farmer's overalls streaked with the toil of labor and the grit of the earth has become the quilt block I sewed onto the pattern instead of onto another quilt piece.

What once was the blue jumper of a baby's first Easter Sunday has become the first piece of the quilt that I stitched by hand that got grandma's approval.

Grandma's new quilt holds pieces of our shared memories . . . memories of success and frustration . . . memories of laughter and tears . . . memories of dreams shared and sheltered by love . . . memories of grandma's aged faith and my fledgling faith . . . memories . . . memories of time shared.

the peanut butter

Grandma taught me the art of quilting, but the memories of quilting with grandma are memories of a time spent with someone I love doing something we both loved to do. While it may be easier to allow our children to spend time engaged in modern, up-to-date recreational pursuits, there is a tremendous value in encouraging our children to take the time to journey back to their parent's or grandparent's world.

Listening to granddad tell stories about his youth or helping grandma prepare a pie creates bonds between the generations. Through discipline, love, thoughtfulness, patience, and kindness, a younger generation can learn to enjoy sharing experiences with someone from another time and place. What a wonderful gift we can give our children through helping them learn that shared stories, time, and experiences create bonds and love in families.

Our parents and grandparents blazed the trail that created the lives our children now enjoy. Through honoring our parents and grandparents, we are teaching our children a Biblical principle. In Ephesians 6:1-3, we are told, "Children, obey your parents in the Lord, for this is right. Honor your father and mother—which is the first commandment with a promise—that it may go well with you and that you may enjoy long life on earth."

Part of honoring my grandma was choosing the leftover quilt blocks. Today, I have a wonderful reminder of my quilting experiences with grandma all wrapped up in one representative quilt. Admittedly, the quilt is not perfect, it has flaws. Few things in life are perfect. A flawed quilt is a great reminder that none of us is perfect. Our perfection is found in a relationship with our Heavenly father (2 Cor. 12:9).

–ADAPTED FROM
RANDALL MORRIS

the jelly

1. When you were growing up, you may have heard your parents tell stories about their upbringing. Try to recall one of these stories and how it impacted your perception of your parents.

2. As our parents age and need more assistance, it becomes more difficult at times to honor their wishes. Our parents frequently want to remain independent when they no longer have the ability to care for themselves. In what ways can we continue to honor our parents even when we have to make decisions concerning their care that they may not like?

3. What activities can you encourage your children to participate in with your parents that will help your children learn more about their grandparents and learn to honor their grandparents?

4. As you age, how do you hope your children will honor you?

the bread

Honor your father and your mother,
as the Lord your God has commanded you,
so that you may live long
and that it may go well with you
in the land the Lord your God is giving you.

–DEUTERONOMY 5:16

To touch the soul
of another human being
is to walk on holy ground.

–Stephen Covey

9
now i lay me
down to
sleep

To be a Christian without prayer is no more possible than to be alive without breathing.

–Martin Luther King Jr.

"Now I lay me down to sleep.
I pray the Lord my soul to keep.
If I should die before I wake
I pray the Lord my soul to take."

The trusting words of a child's prayer, words that may not be understood by the child praying, a prayer that has special meaning for me, a prayer that reflects a longing to go home. Granddad taught me about longing to go home.

After living in Stinnett for three years, granddad is admitted to the hospital because of breathing difficulties. Despite all the changes the stroke created in granddad, he is still my granddad.

Granddad's hospital stay scares me a little, but I reassure myself that he was in the hospital three years before and he didn't die. I know things are worse though. A part of me wants to go see granddad, but another part of me doesn't want to go see him.

One afternoon after school, mom drives me to the hospital, then leads me through the front doors of the hospital. Our shoes click and echo on the tile floor as we walk down the corridor. I purposely stay a step behind mom. I don't have good memories of staying at the hospital with granddad immediately after his stroke. Since granddad was in the hospital for several weeks, all the available adults and older grandkids took turns sitting with granddad in the hospital.

I remember

. . . the antiseptic smell
. . . the discomfort I felt with the responsibility of sitting
with granddad
. . . the confusion I felt when his eyes opened wide without
any recognition
. . . the shock at hearing my granddad cussing at God, the
nurses, even me
. . . the fear I had that granddad would die while I was sit-
ting with him and somehow it would be my fault.

In the time that my granddad lived in Stinnett, many of the terrifying aspects of sitting with granddad in the hospital immediately after his stroke subsided. I stayed with granddad regularly. Staying with granddad has taught me a whole new set of skills.

As I walk into the hospital this time, I know

. . . the stroke changed granddad and he doesn't realize he cusses at us
. . . mom needs help to roll granddad to one side of the bed, so she can change his sheets
. . . granddad needs assistance with a urinal and bedpan
. . . granddad knows who I am and still loves me
. . . I can calm granddad down when he gets agitated
. . . granddad still has his faith and his relationship with God.

I know it sounds strange to put cussing and a relationship with God in the same context. I'm sure it is strange. Yet I believed it as a teenager, and I still believe it today. Granddad was an electrician and spent a great deal of his life on construction sites where profanity was used regularly. Granddad heard a lot of profanity because of his work, but I've never heard anyone say they heard granddad speak a word of profanity until after his stroke. The doctors told my mom that a stroke can cause drastic personality changes.

The cussing was a drastic change. Granddad would cuss when he was agitated, when he was hurt, when someone had to move him, and when someone shaved him. He cussed a lot when mom shaved him. Eventually, mom and dad both had to work together to shave granddad. Dad would hold granddad's hands, so granddad wouldn't hit mom while she shaved him.

There are all of those memories of granddad cussing.

But there are other memories.

When I would sit with granddad, lots of times he would begin quoting Scripture or praying to God out loud. I hadn't heard a lot of spontaneous, random prayers in my life before the stroke.

Most of the prayers I'd heard in my life had been bookends to events

. . . a prayer before Bible class

. . . a prayer to end church
. . . a prayer before starting to eat
. . . a prayer to end the day.

The prayers I heard all my life had been carefully orchestrated events before the stroke. Before the stroke, granddad's prayers were orchestrated.

Since the stroke, granddad's prayers aren't orchestrated at all. His prayers are intimate conversations. His prayers are words uttered to a friend and a companion in a difficult time. He talks to God as if God is in the room with him. Sometimes his voice chokes out whispered prayers; other times, his voice begs for forgiveness.

Life with granddad remains unpredictable. Granddad's prayers are not bookends to events; they are punctuation marks in the midst of events.

. . . Cussing
. . . Prayers whispered during a lonely night
. . . Cussing
. . . Prayers thanking God for blessings
. . . Cussing
. . . Prayers shouted during pain
. . . Cussing
. . . Prayers begging for release from the bondage of paralysis

Eventually, even the unpredictability has its own flow. In that flow of dichotomy between cussing and prayers, I learn great lessons about grace, love, and intimacy with God.

The newest hospital stay interrupts this flow—it threatens the interactions I have with my granddad. As I follow my mom down the sterile hospital corridor, I don't know what to expect.

The echoes of our shoes clicking on the floor are greeted by the muted sounds of screams and groans as we get closer to granddad's room. Mom's demeanor tenses as she realizes the screaming is coming from granddad's room. She turns and puts a hand on my arm.

"Wait here," she says and points to a chair in the hallway.

"Okay," I say and sit obediently in the chair.

As I sit on the chair, I hear granddad screaming.

"Jesus, dear Jesus."

There is a pause.

"I want to come home, dear Jesus."

Granddad's voice rages with desperation.

"Jesus, please release me from this body."

The pleas continue to echo down the hall.

"I want to come home, dear Jesus."

Granddad begs God to let him die . . . Not a quiet bedtime prayer, but a screaming prayer of supplication, a pleading, a begging to come home.

Eventually mom and grandma calm granddad down and he falls asleep.

I don't get to see granddad. Instead, I sit in the chair outside his room praying, praying that God will let granddad come home.

My prayer and granddad's prayer are answered a few days later.

Granddad goes home. I learn that going home is better than staying in this world.

Later, when I hear a child's simple prayer,

"Now I lay me down to sleep,
I pray the Lord my soul to keep,
If I should die before I wake,
I pray the Lord my soul to take."

I remember that God answers prayers.

the peanut butter

The ravages of disease are often times shocking. Sometimes just the aging process itself reminds us that we are not as nimble as we once were. We think more about our mortality than we once did. We actually realize there are some things we used to do without any problem that become more of a challenge. Our memory is not as sharp as it once was.

God knows and understands our human frailties better than we do. His power is made perfect in our weaknesses (2 Cor. 12:9). When a stroke attacks the part of the brain that governs rational thought and protects us from rash speech and action, God knows and understands. He knows that the brain has been injured and that what is said and done is not us, but the brain injury. Just as he would not expect a crippled man to run or a blind man to marvel at a sunset, He would not hold a stroke victim accountable for words spoken or attitudes displayed that were not a part of the whole being when he was rational and uninjured.

Even when we are well and act out in ways that are contrary to our training in the Scriptures, He knows our heart. He knows if and when our remorse is sincere; our repentance is genuine; our efforts at reform are authentic. God always forgives, and never grows weary of doing so—as long as we never give up the fight against sin; as long as we never get discouraged or dissuaded from seeking His mercy; as long as our demeanor and emphasis of life continues to be one of obedience.

Peter was told, and we all should remember "the spirit is willing, but the body is weak" (Matt. 26:40-41). God knows that and deals with us accordingly. We need to remember it as well and do as commanded to "Watch and pray that we enter not into temptation;" seek to strengthen ourselves against temptation (Eph. 6:10-18); and ask forgiveness when we succumb to temptation (1 John 1:7-9).

–ADAPTED FROM RANDALL MORRIS

the jelly

1. In caring for your parents or grandparents, what changes in their health have been the most difficult for you to deal with? Why?

2. In the midst of caring for our loved ones, it is often difficult to accept their health challenges. How have changes in your parents' health challenged your faith?

3. What do you fear most about aging yourself?

4. What do you hope your children learn from seeing the health challenges your parents or grandparents are facing?

the bread

In the same way,
the Spirit helps us in our weakness.
We do not know what we ought to pray for,
but the Spirit himself intercedes for us
with groans that words cannot express.

–ROMANS 8:26

Prayer is not asking. It is a longing of the soul.

It is daily admission of one's weakness.

It is better in prayer to have a heart

without words than words without a heart.

–Mahatma Gandhi

The wish to pray is a prayer in itself.

–Georges Bernanos

Expect to have hope rekindled.
Expect your prayers
to be answered in wondrous ways.
The dry seasons in life do not last.
The spring rains will come again.

–Sarah Ban Breathnach

10
recipe for respect

Being brilliant is no great feat

if you respect nothing.

–Johann Wolfgang von Goethe

My family serves Mexican Casserole for Christmas Dinner on New Year's Day. The Mexican Casserole and Christmas Dinner on New Year's Day are fundamental traditions in my family. The recipe for Mexican Casserole requires the following:

* Brown two pounds of ground beef in large skillet.

* Add one onion. Do not brown onion.

* Add one can of mushroom soup, one can of hot chilies, one can of enchilada sauce, and one cup of water.

* Add a dash of garlic salt.

* Mix well.

* Heat in skillet until mixture begins to boil.

* Remove from heat.

* Grate one pound of cheese.

* Layer meat mixture, corn tortillas, and grated cheese until all ingredients are gone.

* Cook at 350 degrees for 20 minutes.

* Serve with loving hands.

A simple, yet effective recipe.

While the Mexican Casserole is served at other meals, it is most closely associated with our New Year's Day Christmas Dinner. Every year, my mom, my grandma, and my cousin collaborate on the menu and divide up responsibilities. In recent years, grandma's ability to hold up her end of the menu has been steadily declining. Even when she tries to contribute to our regular family meals, she struggles.

Grandma still spends hours in the kitchen every day. Like an aging general trying to commandeer troops, grandma rallies all her efforts to exert control over the domain she used to govern. She still cooks with no net. Recipes rarely offer guidance.

Grandma's hands once effortlessly flew through kitchen cabinets retrieving ingredients, bowls, spoons, and pans. Now her hands move slowly with concerted effort. Hands that once deftly arranged ingredients in layers and bowls move with hesitation and stiffness. Once a handful of this, a pinch of that, and a dab of fat synchronized in unique dance steps. Now a handful of this, a pinch of that, and a dab of fat rebel and ruin grandma's cooking efforts. The ad lib style of cooking that distinguished grandma for years as an excellent cook now defeats grandma's creations.

Not that I blame grandma. Her senses betray her. Her eyes no longer distinguish between the jars, canisters, and ingredients. Her taste buds no longer distinguish between salt and sugar. Her nose no longer distinguishes between just done and just burned. Grandma has spent a lifetime immersed in an identity as a distinguished cook. Her competence and self-worth tie into her ability to feed others. During her lifetime, grandma has relied on her cooking to generate words of praise and expressions of appreciation. Now her cooking competence abandons her.

Mom's recognition of grandma's declining cooking skills sandwiches her between two generations—between meeting the needs of her parents and meeting the needs of her children. Mom understands how important cooking is to grandma's sense of competence and identity. While mom recognizes that grandma's food can be distasteful to eat, she also understands how important it is to teach her children to be respectful and kind toward others. In response to grandma's declining cooking competencies, mom develops a new set of dinner table rules.

Rule 1: Everyone at the table takes at least one serving of any dish grandma prepares. (The one serving has to be of a normal size. No miniature servings are allowed.)

Rule 2: Everyone at the table has to eat at least one serving of any dish grandma prepares. (This rule was initiated in response to those of us who would just creatively move food around on our plates rather than eating it.)

Rule 3: Everyone at the table has to thank grandma for bringing food to the meal and (when applicable) tell her how good it tasted. (We weren't expected to lie, but if she fixed a dish that tasted normal, we were expected to compliment her cooking.)

Mom's rules of respect for grandma's cooking were enforced with an ironclad determination. When I would grimace about Jell-O made with salt instead of sugar, mom would give me the warning look. When I heroically choked down gummy sweet potatoes, mom would give me a nod of approval. When I would take a small helping of beans, mom would give me another opportunity to take more beans.

Grandma's declining cooking abilities reach a pinnacle of hazard during New Year's Day Christmas Dinner. Mom calls all of us to gather around grandma's oak pedestal table. Each of us becomes a link in a chain as we grasp hands and bow our heads in prayer. Once the "Amen" resounds, the platters and bowls of food march from hand to hand.

As the Mexican casserole proceeds around the table, stunned expressions plaster on faces. When I dip the serving spoon into the casserole and deposit a serving on my plate, I immediately identify the problem. Uncooked hamburger meat nestles in the cheese and tortillas of the casserole dish. I take a deep breath, raise my eyebrows, and pass the Mexican casserole to the next person.

I remember the rules. I've never eaten raw meat before, but grandma "cooked" (can you really say she cooked a raw-meat casserole?) the Mexican Casserole. The rules apply.

Before I take a bite of the casserole, grandma gets up from the table to check on rolls in the oven. While her back is turned, we all gesture and grimace about the raw meat. Mom gestures for us to settle down and shakes her head "no." She then silently mouths the words "You don't have to eat it." Visible relief engulfs the table.

Yet mom has ingrained the rules.

Rule 1: Everyone at the table takes at least one serving of any dish grandma prepares.

Rule 2: Everyone at the table has to eat at least one serving of any dish grandma prepares.

Rule 3: Everyone at the table has to thank grandma for bringing food to the meal.

Without any verbal communication, we decide collectively that we can't violate the intent of the rules. While none of us is willing to eat raw meat, we want to be respectful and kind to grandma. An interesting conspiracy begins to unfold.

The next time grandma gets up from the table, my sister rakes her casserole into a planter. Once my brother sees what my sister is doing, he rakes his casserole in the trashcan. Normal conversation at the table continues as everyone recognizes what is happening. For the rest of the meal, the conversation flows without interruptions when grandma leaves the table as we pass and trade plates, then rake Mexican casserole into napkins, trash cans, and planters. At that point, we had learned more than mom's dinner table rules, we had learned a recipe for respect. The recipe requires the following:

* Bring an aging grandparent into the daily lives of four teens.

* Add one set of sandwiched parents.

* Add two jobs, extra curricular activities, and church responsibilities.

* Add a dash of humor.

* Mix well.

* Teach values until they stick.

* Remove from negative influences.

* Give daily doses of Bible study.

* Layer rules, respect, and compassion.

* Let children mature.

* Serve with loving hands.

A simple, yet effective recipe.

the peanut butter

Showing respect to others has become an uncommon practice in our society. It is not just disrespect for the aged or parents. Our culture has lost respect for authority figures, school administrators, bosses, even the police. There is a general lack of respect for our peers, and even for one's self. Our cultural lack of respect for others stands in contrast to the Biblical command to "show proper respect to everyone" (1 Pet. 2:17). In Leviticus, we are instructed to "rise in the presence of the aged, show respect for the elderly and revere your God" (Lev. 19:32).

A wonderful example of respect is found in Exodus 18:7-8. Moses is a respected leader of a great nation. He has a lot of power and status, yet we see Moses get on the ground and bow before his father-in-law Jethro. Moses, a great man of public stature and power, humbles himself by bowing. Moses then proceeds to kiss Jethro showing even more respect for the man. However, the display of respect didn't stop there. Amidst all the business of leading a demanding nation through the desert, Moses takes time out of his busy day to invite his elderly father-in-law to enter his tent and discuss all the events that had happened since the last time they had been together. The great powerful leader Moses showed humility in the presence of the elderly by bowing at his feet, Moses showed great respect by kissing him, and even showed greater respect by putting aside time to sit and spend time with him.

Parents have a difficult task in teaching respect in our society. Parents often stand alone in setting rules that have as their only purpose protecting the dignity of another human being. Through establishing rules for respecting my grandma, my parents taught all of us that every soul is valuable in God's kingdom and that everyone deserves to be treated with the respect due to a child of God.

the jelly

1. Describe how your parents taught you to respect others and to treat others with compassion.

2. Describe how other people have shown you respect. How did you feel about being treated respectfully?

3. How can you teach your children to treat your parents or grandparents with the patience and compassion that Moses displayed in his interactions with Jethro?

4. How can you teach your children to respect God's laws and teachings?

the bread

*Do nothing out
of selfish ambition or vain conceit,
but in humility consider others
better than yourselves.
Each of you should look
not only to your own interests,
but also to the interests of others.
Your attitude should be the same
as that of Christ Jesus.*

–PHILIPPIANS 2:3-5

This is the final test of a gentleman:

his respect for those

who can be of no possible service to him.

–William Lyon Phelps

We are apt to forget that children watch examples

better than they listen to preaching.

–Roy L. Smith

11

grandma's blessing

Children will not remember you
for the material things you provided
but for the feeling that you cherished them.

–Richard L. Evans

Snow lines the side of the road as I drive into the parking lot of the nursing home where my grandma is staying. It's the day after Christmas and I'm stopping by to leave a Christmas gift with grandma. I'm rushing to get back home. I glance at my watch as I rush through the doors of the nursing home. If I don't delay too long, I'll be able to get home in time to get a few errands done.

As much as I love my grandma, I don't want to stay at the nursing home any longer than I absolutely have to. The sounds, smells, and sights of the nursing home are foreign and a little bit frightening. I negotiate the maze of wheelchairs and walkers in the foyer and make a quick right turn down the hall to grandma's room. Just as I reach the door, I stop for a second.

I need a second, a second to remember . . . the afternoons spent picking out quilt pieces or baking pies in her kitchen . . . grandma's aimless way of wandering through her house and yard . . . evenings spent drinking grape juice and eating vanilla ice cream . . . the adventure of taking her grocery shopping on Wednesdays.

I need a second, a second to prepare myself . . . for how vulnerable and helpless grandma seems . . . for recognizing that a part of grandma is no longer there . . . for accepting that opportunities to talk with grandma are gone.

I need a second, a second to recognize that the grandma I know is gone.

When I peek around the corner into her room, I smile as I see a familiar quilt. The quilt is tattered and worn from being washed too many times. Years earlier grandma had pieced that quilt herself. Quilting with grandma is one of the memories I cherish most from my childhood. I remember the slant of the sun coming through the window as daylight faded, and we were trying to get the last pieces of fabric cut out for the quilt. I can still feel grandma's hand on my shoulder as she bent over me to supervise my first stitches. I remember our lively debates about which fabrics would become a part of our creation.

As I stand at the foot of grandma's bed in the nursing home, it is comforting to see her lying beneath one of her quilts. For several minutes, I lean against the door because grandma is asleep. Her eyes shut out the world, and her breath rasps evenly from her body. I don't want to wake her. I wonder if I will even get to see her today. After a few minutes, grandma seems to sense my presence. Her eyes flutter open. A startled and slightly disoriented look crosses her face. She looks like a small child waking up in an unfamiliar room as her eyes search the room looking for something she recognizes. Regrettably, grandma has days now when she doesn't recognize anything or anyone.

I take a deep breath and hope against hope that this will be a good day—a day when grandma will know who I am.

"Hi, Grandma! I'm Beth, your granddaughter," I say.

Grandma turns her head and watches with a puzzled expression as I walk to her bedside.

"Honey . . . I'm sorry . . . who are you?" a wavering voice responds.

"It's Beth, Grandma. I'm Geneva's daughter."

"You're Beth?" questions grandma.

"Yes, Grandma, I'm Beth."

Grandma is still searching for some connection. "What do you do honey?"

"I teach school, Grandma."

Grandma sighs and says, "School teachin' is good."

I don't know how to respond. Silence hangs between us for an uncomfortable moment; then grandma asks, "Are you still living with your parents?"

"No, I live in Amarillo." At this point, I feel certain that my grandma still doesn't know who I am. I decide to leave her Christmas gift and get out of the room as quickly as I can. I see no purpose in continuing the conversation.

"Grandma, I brought you a present." I hold out a box in the direction of her bed, and explain, "It's a new gown. See, it's your favorite color, pink." I personally think that a gown is a lame gift for someone in a nursing home, but I didn't know what else to bring.

Grandma doesn't seem to think it is a lame gift. Her face lights up, and her voice seems stronger when she responds, "I love pink things. Honey, put that in the top drawer. I like to know where things are."

"It's in the top drawer," I assure her as I walk over to the dresser. I know in five minutes she won't remember seeing me or the gown I gave her.

By the time I walk back over to the bed, grandma's eyes are sliding shut. Silence surrounds grandma for a few minutes, then the steady hum of her breathing fills the quietness of the room. The innocence of childhood floods her face as sleep shrouds her age. I realize this is my opportunity to make a quick exit, but memories mesmerize me. Grandma's face unclouded by confusion triggers warm memories of laughter and haunting memories of frustration. I stand beside her bed, torn between hope—hope that the grandma I remember will awaken—and fear—fear that the grandma who dozed off will awaken. The tug-of-war between hope and fear continues as sadness drapes over me. I miss grandma. When the sadness creeps to the far reaches of my soul, I stand up to leave. Grieving the living is beyond my strength. As I reach the end of the bed, I look back at grandma's face one more time. Surprisingly, her eyes flutter open.

My fear is confirmed as a puzzled expression slides across grandma's face and she says, "Honey . . . I'm sorry . . . I think I know you . . . who are you?"

I give the same response I'd given a few minutes earlier, "It's Beth, Grandma. I'm Geneva's daughter."

Grandma repeats her earlier question "You're Beth?"

"Yes, Grandma, I'm Beth," I respond again.

As grandma searches my face looking for a connection, I recognize that we are replaying our first conversation verbatim. Grandma's next question confirms my assumption.

"What do you do honey?" she asks.

"I teach school, Grandma," I reply again.

Grandma sighs and says again, "School teachin' is good."

Once again silence hangs between us for a moment, then grandma asks, "Are you still living with your parents?"

I marvel at the exact precision of grandma's mirrored conversation. Even the pauses and silences are identical. I continue to parrot my earlier responses.

"No, I live in Amarillo," I say.

In a few minutes grandma drifts off to sleep for a second time. Oddly enough, I find myself sitting down in the chair again. I wait for her to awaken. Eventually, her eyes open again and a puzzled expression crosses her face. The conversation begins again.

"Honey . . . I'm sorry . . . I think I know you . . . who are you?"

The answer is the same. The conversation continues precisely. We both respond exactly as before until grandma drifts off again. My mind tells me that repeating the same conversation should be frustrating, but my heart finds the uncomplicated, simple exchange comforting. I want to be here with grandma. I recognize that an odd sort of turn about is occurring. When I was a young child, I asked grandma the same questions over and over and over again. Now it was her turn to ask the questions and my turn to be patient.

The ritual continues, and I stay the entire afternoon. As daylight fades, I know I have to leave. Once again grandma repeats her question about who I am.

"Honey . . . I'm sorry . . . I think I know you . . . who are you?"

"It's Beth, Grandma. I'm Geneva's daughter," I hesitate for a moment in the familiar rhythm of the conversation, but quickly plunge ahead before grandma can continue the pattern. "Grandma, I have to leave now. I'll be back to see you in a week or two."

Grandma seems unaware that I've changed the rhythm of our pattern and interjected a finale to our conversation.

She continues as though the conversation is unchanged and says, "You're Beth?"

Suddenly, grandma's face changes.

Her blue eyes fill with light and a smile slowly spreads across her face. She unwraps her hand from the quilt and takes my hand in hers.

"Honey, I love you so much," she says.

I hold her fragile hand . . . the hand that helped me piece my first quilt . . . found Bible verses in church for me . . . slapped my hand when I reached for too many cookies . . . held my hand when I needed a friend. I hold on to everything we shared and everything we are losing at that moment.

I bend over and hug grandma.

"I love you too, Grandma," I reply as tears run down my cheeks.

Grandma's eyes close again.

I tiptoe out of her room.

Nine days later, grandma dies. I never see her again.

Even now, years later, I can hear her say, "Honey, I love you so much."

I see her eyes light up with recognition and love.

I feel the warmth of her hand wrapped around my hand.

Grandma's blessing beats back time and embraces me when she can no longer hold my hand.

the peanut butter

"Honey, I love you so much" have been words of validation for decades for me. When I am feeling worn down, worn out, or overwhelmed, I remember my grandma's eyes lighting up with recognition and love.

Validation. An acknowledgment from someone you admire, respect, love that you are a worthy person. Worthy to know, talk to, be admired in return. Every human being needs validation.

In Matthew 3 Jesus comes to John to be baptized. After His baptism God validates Jesus before all who are present, saying, "This is my Son, whom I love; with him I am well pleased" (Matt. 3:17).

In Matthew 17, Jesus, Moses, and Elijah appear before Peter, James and John. Peter proposes to honor this occasion with the building of three tabernacles: one for Jesus, one for Moses and one for Elijah. Immediately, Elijah and Moses fade from the scene, Jesus alone remains, and the voice of God from heaven says, "This is my Son, whom I love; with him I am well pleased. Listen to him!" (Matt. 17:5). Before three witnesses, and by their testimony before the entire world, the heavenly Father validates His Son Jesus as the one and only voice to hear and heed.

God saw the importance of validating His Son because validation is the lifeblood of self-respect and self esteem—and the esteem and respect we seek from and receive from others. It is a red-letter day when someone acknowledges to you and especially in the presence of others, "You've done all right."

Even in the lips of one who has long since escaped from the present world into a past world, where the present is less real than memories; where memories have faded, recognition is dimmed, even then at the close of the day, at the close of life "I love you so much, honey" is such a validation of our worth as a person that it feeds our soul for decades.

–ADAPTED FROM RANDALL MORRIS

the jelly

1. Describe ways your parents and others have validated you doing your lifetime.

2. How can you continue to provide validation for your aging parents or grandparents?

3. How can you provide validation for your children?

4. How can you teach your children that the ultimate validation must come from their heavenly Father?

the bread

Love is patient, love is kind.

It does not envy,

it does not boast,

it is not proud.

It is not rude,

it is not self-seeking,

it is not easily angered,

it keeps no record of wrongs.

Love does not delight in evil

but rejoices with the truth.

It always protects,

always trusts,

always hopes,

always perseveres.

Love never fails.

–1 CORINTHIANS 13: 4-8

Nobody can do for little children

what grandparents do.

Grandparents sort of sprinkle stardust

over the lives of little children.

–Alex Haley

12

taking
my turn

Other things may change us,
but we start and end with family.

–Anthony Brandt

*N*ight falls. Time for me to go to bed. I dread sleep.

Mom takes my hand and walks me to my room. She hugs me, tucks the sheets around me and kisses me. When mom turns to leave, I watch her reach over and flip the light switch off.

Fear and panic wash over me. During the last week, I've been having a recurring nightmare. I've talked to my mom several times about the dream. She told me that I didn't have to be afraid of a dream because it is not real. I scold myself for being fearful, but the fear stays with me.

Now as I lie in my bed, I feel small and afraid. I want my mom to wrap her arms around me and calmly reassure me that everything will be all right, but I know I have to stay in bed and conquer my fears.

Darkness bathes my room. I lie in bed staring straight ahead at the ceiling and willing myself to have courage. I can't see anything for several minutes while my eyes adjust to the darkness. Eventually I make out the dark outlines of my furniture. I tense my muscles and lie rigid in the bed. I'm determined to resist the sleepiness that washes over me.

I dread sleep. Sleep escorts dreams into my world. I toss and turn and fight sleep. Darkness is all I can see or feel. I am alone fighting the unknown. Despite my efforts, eventually sleep closes in around me. The darkness surrounds me.

In the middle of the night, my wheezing gasps rupture the silence of the darkness. The wheezing becomes louder.

"Mom, Mom," I cry out into the darkness. I wait alone and terrified in the blanket of darkness.

A gentle light in the hallway breaks the darkness. Light bathes the open doorway of my room. I hear the even tempo of socked feet marching down the hall. I turn expectantly toward the door.

A silhouette of a woman is framed in the doorway. The soft curves of the silhouette exude the comfort of a familiar form. The woman quietly enters my room and makes her way to my bedside. She sits down on the edge of the bed. I look into a face shadowed in darkness. Suddenly, I know something is wrong. I push the woman away.

"You're not my mom. Turn the lights on. Go away. I want my

mom. Turn the lights on," I scream.

The woman reaches across to try to comfort me. I withdraw into the corner of the bed as far away from her as I can get. My terrified screams echo through the darkness.

"I want my mom. Mom, come here. Turn the light on. I want my mom," I scream hysterically.

The woman reluctantly rises and walks back toward the light in the hallway. When she reaches the doorway, she flips the light switch. Light immediately overpowers the darkness. The woman in my room is a stranger.

I sit up in the bed, screaming for my mom.

The dream seems so real.

My eyes open. Darkness greets me.

Just before the terror engulfs me, my mom wraps her arms around me and calmly reassures me that everything is going to be all right. She pushes my fear out of the room.

"Everything is okay. You need to wake up," she gently urges me, "Wake up and we'll have a tea party." She reaches over, picks me up, and cradles me like a baby while she shakes my shoulder to wake me. I snuggle against the warmth of her body while she carries me to the kitchen. Gradually I begin to breathe easier.

Mom sits me in one of the chairs at the table while she puts water in the kettle to heat. As the water heats in the kettle, mom mixes tea, lemon and honey together in cups for each of us. Waiting for the water to heat, mom distracts me with chatter about the previous day's events. When the whistle on the kettle begins to screech, mom efficiently removes it from the stove. The screeching whistle falls silent before it rouses anyone else from the oblivion of sleep. Mom adds the boiling water to our tea cups and hands me one cup then cradles the other cup in her own hands. The warmth of the teacup and mom's love cradle me. We indulge in a few quiet minutes of chatter as we drink at our private midnight tea party.

Only too quickly, mom reaches for my teacup and announces, "It's time for you to get back in bed young lady. Morning will be here before you know it."

I push away from the table and reach for my mom's extended

hand. Mom takes my hand and walks me to my room. She hugs me, tucks the sheets around me and kisses me.

Darkness bathes the room.
I snuggle into the blankets.
Calmness settles over me.
Mom is taking care of me.

Decades later, day dawns. Time for me to see mom. I dread the unknown.

I watch the clock tick off the minutes until 10:00 a.m. I'm standing outside the ICU, and I'm not sure what I'll find on the other side of the doors. Late last night, my dad called and told me that my mom was in ICU with a brain hemorrhage. I'd gotten up early this morning to drive the two hours to the hospital to see my mother during the first visitation time.

Guilt and panic wash over me. During the last week, I'd talked to my mom several times. She'd told me she wasn't feeling well and complained about headaches. In fact, she hadn't felt well in over two weeks. I'd talked to dad on Saturday and he'd agreed to take her to the doctor yesterday. I scold myself for not taking the time out of my schedule to drive up and check on her earlier in the week.

Now as I stand outside the ICU, I feel much too young and afraid to deal with the situation. I want to turn back time. I want my mom to wrap her arms around me and calmly reassure me that everything is going to be all right. I want to hear the whistle of the kettle and feel the warmth of a teacup in my hands. I want the familiar setting of the kitchen and the tradition of a shared midnight tea party to push away my fear. Without the comfort of my mom's arms, I want to run.

A sterile brightness bathes the waiting room. I sit in a chair staring straight ahead at the wall and willing myself to have courage. I'm looking without seeing anything. I am willing myself to act like an adult, not like the child I think I am. The doors of the ICU swing open with a thud. I take a deep breath. I'm an adult. Adults don't run away. Adults don't crawl under the blankets and hide from the dark. Adults get out of bed and turn on the light.

I stand up and walk through the doors and down the hall to the nurses' station in ICU. I am determined to resist the panic that washes over me. I dread what I might find when I see my mom. The sterile brightness of the ICU surrounds me, but I feel alone in the darkness.

When I reach the nurses' station, I ask, "Where's Geneva Robinson?"

The nurse points to the room directly in front of the nurses' station. A nurse perches at a table just outside the curtain separating my mom from the other patients in ICU. I push the curtain aside and slip into my mom's room. A nurse stands between my mom and me. The nurse checks the bag hanging on the IV pole and then reaches over and straightens the pillows under my mom's head.

I stand to one side of the foot of the bed.

I can't see my mom's face.

Mom can't see my face.

I wonder if she will recognize my face when she sees me. Will she know who I am? Will my mom still be there when I look into her eyes? Will she remember our ritual of midnight tea parties? Will she remember to keep me safe in the dark? Will she remember to chase the cold away?

The nurse moves away. I see my mom's eyes. Tears begin to stream down her face. She hesitates for a moment then says, "I'm so sorry."

I walk over to mom's bed and take her hand in my hands.

"Sorry for what, Mom?"

"I'm supposed to take care of you. You're not supposed to take care of me."

"Mom, you've taken care of me for thirty-five years, I think maybe it's time for me to take care of you."

The tears continue to flow down mom's face. I hug my mom, tuck the sheets around her, and kiss her forehead.

Sterile light bathes the room.
Mom is snuggled into hospital blankets.
Calmness settles over me.
Mom has taken care of me.
Now, it is my turn to take care of her.

the peanut butter

Being fearful and overwhelmed are ordinary parts of life. Christians are not insulated from the dread and anxieties of life, but have resources available to reconstitute calmness and peace. Think about the incident in Matthew 8, when "Jesus got into a boat and his disciples followed him. Without warning, a furious storm came up on the lake, so that the waves swept over the boat." The disciples knew where to go. They went to awaken Jesus, and Jesus calmed the storm (vv. 23-26). His response was simple, direct, and immediate.

We need to learn as the disciples did: that in times of peril, we need to focus our attention on the Lord. Consider Matthew 14, when the disciples see Jesus walking on the water, and again are frightened. He reassures them saying, "Take courage! It is I. Don't be afraid" (v. 27). Peter's confidence soars, and he requests permission to walk on water with the Jesus, which he does, if only briefly, until he is gripped with fear again. But even in this second moment of despair, he calls for Jesus' help and is not denied, as we read, Jesus "reached out his hand and caught him." (v. 31). Obviously, the strong hand of the Lord is ready to grasp us and snatch us free from danger.

A strong arm, a reassuring voice, a history of rescue and redemption will give us confidence and reassurance when we are frightened. Sometimes it is the older, wiser and stronger parent or mentor assuring us it will be all right; finding simple ways, like midnight tea parties, to assuage our bedtime fears. Then, as years pass by, those who once saved us from our nightmares encounter their own uncertainties and we repay them for reassuring us with many of the same techniques they so ably endowed us with.

But for the faithful child of God we have the reassurance

of the Master, and best summarized by Paul, saying, "Do not be anxious about anything, but in everything, by prayer and petition, with thanksgiving, present your requests to God. And the peace of God, which transcends all understanding, will guard your hearts and your minds in Christ Jesus" (Phil. 4:6-7).

–ADAPTED FROM RANDALL MORRIS

the jelly

1. How do you remember your parents calming your fears and helping you feel safe when you were a child?

2. Describe situations you have faced in caring for your parents when you felt frightened or overwhelmed. How did you deal with feeling frightened or overwhelmed?

3. What do you do to help your children deal with their fears and anxieties?

4. How do you hope your children will deal with feeling afraid and overwhelmed when they are adults?

The Lord is my light and my salvation—
whom shall I fear?
The Lord is the stronghold of my life—
of whom shall I be afraid?
When evil men advance against me
to devour my flesh,
when my enemies and my foes attack me,
they will stumble and fall.
Though an army besiege me,
my heart will not fear;
though war break out against me,
even then will I be confident.

–PSALMS 27:1-3

the bread

*The L*ord *bless you and keep you;*
*the L*ord *make his face shine*
upon you and be gracious to you;
the LORD turn his face
toward you and give you peace.

–NUMBERS 6:24-26

The Lord bless you and keep you;

the Lord make his face shine

upon you and be gracious to you;

the Lord turn his face

toward you and give you peace.

–Numbers 6:24-26

about the author

Dr. Beth Robinson is currently a Professor of Psychology and Chair of the Department of Behavioral Sciences at Lubbock Christian University in Texas. Dr. Robinson is a licensed professional counselor, an approved supervisor for licensed professional counselors, and a certified school counselor. She has written *Sex: Helping Church Teens Deal With Challenging Issues* and numerous articles for publication in professional journals. Along with L.J. Bradley and E. Jarchow, she authored the book *All about Sex: The School Counselor's Guide to Handling Tough Adolescent Problems.*

She is in constant demand as a speaker and trainer in universities and churches across the country. In addition, she frequently serves as a consultant to congregations on issues related to counseling and working with teens and children in churches. She has been active in both church ministry and community service.

Dr. Robinson lives in Lubbock, Texas. She lives with Christi, LaTreca, Gerrit, Marcus, Sosa, and Toni.